GETTING READY

Preparing the Church
for the Return of Jesus

DR. DANIEL M. SWEGER

Gazelle
PRESS

ISBN 1-58169-149-1
For Worldwide Distribution
Printed in the U.S.A.

Gazelle Press
P.O. Box 191540 • Mobile, AL 36619
800-367-8203

TABLE OF CONTENTS

Preface

How many Christians today believe they understand biblical prophecy concerning the end days, the subject theologians call eschatology? I have asked this question whenever I teach on it, and few respond in the affirmative. Many have not even read the prophetic books of Ezekiel, Daniel, Zechariah, and Revelation.

Part of the problem is that there is little general agreement concerning the interpretation of end-times prophecy. During the 30 years I have been teaching the Bible, I did little teaching on this subject until recently. During that time, I periodically read books on the subject by a variety of authors, such as Hal Lindsey, Arthur Bloomfield, and Hilton Sutton, all who have different approaches. I would read a book or two, and while each one would have certain good points, none seemed to satisfy my desire to have a complete interpretation, so I always put them aside. Like everyone else, I felt I did not quite understand the subject.

I was in Kenya in August 2001, teaching in two different Bible schools and staying in Malindi at the house of missionary friends, Ken and Ibby VanDruff. In my spare time, I picked up a book on prophecy by Marvin Rosenthal, *The Pre-Wrath Rapture of the Church,* that Ken was using for a class he was preparing. As I read it, I said, "Yes! This is a biblical approach." When I got home, I bought my own copy. Subsequently, I found a second book (*The Sign of Christ's Coming and the End of the Age* by Robert Van Kampen), which covered the entire subject of Christ's return in more detail. These two books launched a two-year long study.

This book is the result of that study and of divine

revelation. It is not concerned with the events of the last days; that subject is covered elsewhere (*The Coming Day of the Lord*, available from the author). The focus of this book, however, is what we need to be doing to prepare for Jesus' return, and as such, it is quite practical.

I have taught this subject now in seminar form in both the United States and countries in Africa. The more I prepare to teach, the more I have a sense of urgency. The time is growing short. I do not believe the church, at least in the United States and Africa, is prepared for the coming events. It has been lulled to sleep by well-intentioned, but incorrect, teaching that the church will not have to suffer persecution during the end time. It is my prayer that God will use this book to awaken believers everywhere.

There have been many who have encouraged me over the years, and I would like to thank each one. I especially want to thank Bruce Mitchell and Betty Hertzler for their encouragement.

Finally, this book would not have been possible without the help and support of my wonderful wife Carol. The last couple of years have brought great change, and she has stood with me. Thank you, and I love you.

CHAPTER 1

The Beginning of the Return

*And if I go and prepare a place for you, I will come
again, and receive you to Myself; that where I am
you may be also* (John 14:3).

I t was a dramatic moment. Just 40 days earlier, the
disciples had greeted with skepticism the news that
the tomb was empty and that He had arisen from
the dead. But since that time He had been with them,
talked with them, explained the scriptures to them, and
even had eaten with them. They had touched Him, and
as John said, they "handled" Him. (I John 1:1) There
was no longer a question about His resurrection from
the dead. While His body was different now than it was
before the crucifixion, it was just as real.

He had gathered them together, as usual, and was
telling them to wait for the Holy Spirit, when suddenly
He began to arise from the earth. They watched in awe
as He went up into a cloud, and He was gone. Just like
that! It was unbelievable! They could not take their eyes
away from the cloud; they just stared, with their mouths
hanging wide open.

Then two angels appeared and announced to the disciples that Jesus was going to come back. Not in some
spiritual way, but physically, in the same body, in the
same way, as when He left (Acts 1:1-11).

Jesus is coming back! If there is any one thing we know from prophecy, we know that Jesus is coming back. He promised He would, and so there is absolutely no question. The question, however, that so many ask is, "What will be the circumstances and nature of His return?"

The disciples also wanted to know the answer to that question, and so they asked Jesus, "What will be the sign of Your coming, and of the end of the age?" (Matthew 24: 3)

What follows in Matthew 24:4-31 is a straightforward answer to their question. Since they were sitting on the Mount of Olives at the time, the answer Jesus gave is called the Olivet Discourse, and it can be divided into three distinct parts:

- Matthew 24:4-8—The beginning of the end of the age, which is like birth pangs.
- Matthew 24:9-28—The tribulation and the wrath of Satan.
- Matthew 24:29-31—The return of Jesus.

The Beginning of Birth Pangs

And Jesus answered and said to them, "See to it that no one misleads you. For many will come in My name, saying, 'I am the Christ,' and will mislead many. And you will be hearing of wars and rumors of wars; see that you are not frightened, for those things must take place, but that is not yet the end. For nation will rise against nation, and kingdom against kingdom, and in various places there will be famines and earthquakes. But all these things are merely the beginning of birth pangs (Matthew 24:4-8).

Jesus begins His answer by listing several signs for them to watch.

1. The existence of false christs;
2. Wars and rumors of wars;
3. Famines and earthquakes.

Jesus is the Head of the Church and the only Person worthy of worship. He, and He alone, is the Christ—the Anointed One of God. Jesus is the way, the truth and the life. A false christ is one who puts himself in the place of Jesus, claiming to have truth that supercedes Jesus. There have been many such persons in the centuries of the church, and some, like Mohammed, have been successful in persuading many to follow after them.

Wars abound in our time. A study shows that wars have increased almost exponentially in the last 500 years.[1] With weapons of mass destruction, high-tech weaponry and the means to deliver them over long distances, war takes on a new dimension. As terrible as the atomic bombs were that were dropped on Japan in World War II, they pale in comparison to the nuclear capabilities of more than a dozen nations today. Even terrorist organizations seem to have the ability to deliver mass death almost anywhere in the world.

Conflicts and wars have been around throughout history, so it is not merely the presence of these signs that is important, rather it is their intensity. Just as birth pangs become more intense and frequent as the time approaches for the birth of a baby, so these events will become more pronounced and frequent. As the time approaches for Jesus' return, we can expect an increase in all these things.

The culmination will be the appearance of one false christ who is going to be the final one. Paul calls him "the man of lawlessness...the son of destruction" (II

Thessalonians 2:3). John describes him in Revelation as a beast with seven heads and ten horns who receives great power from Satan (Revelation 13:1-10). This one, to whom many give the title the Antichrist, will achieve world domination and demand worship from all the people of the world for a period of time.

Tribulation, Death, Apostasy

Jesus continued by describing several more things that will happen in the time leading up to His return. As the intensity of the birth pangs will continue to increase, the followers of Jesus will be subjected to a series of pressures. Energized by Satan, the Antichrist will institute a system whereby he will effectively control the peoples of the world. This system has two prongs.

First, true to his title, the Antichrist will declare himself to be god and require that all the people worship him. Satan will empower him through supernatural signs and wonders, and many people will be deceived into believing that he is indeed the savior of the world.

Secondly, he will institute a world economic system, so that no one can perform any financial transaction without becoming a part of his structure.

Tribulation and Death

Then they will deliver you up to tribulation, and will kill you, and you will be hated by all nations on account of My name....For then there will be a great tribulation, such as has not occurred since the beginning of the world until now, nor ever shall (Matthew 24:9, 21).

As Jesus spoke to His disciples, He announced that there would be a time of great persecution. The event that will initiate this tribulation is the "abomination of desolation which was spoken of through Daniel the prophet" (Matthew 24:15; see Daniel 9:27). The abomination of desolation will occur when the Antichrist enters into the Holy of Holies of the Temple in Jerusalem and declares himself to be god.

Jesus further elaborated and said that it would be "a great tribulation, such as has not occurred since the beginning of the world until now, nor ever shall be" (Matthew 24:21). The goal of the Antichrist is to eliminate the people of God, and he will begin in Israel where he will attempt to kill the Jews. That is why the angel tells Daniel, "And there will be a time of distress such as never occurred since there was a nation until [this] time" (Daniel 12:1).

But it will not end there. It will soon spread to all the people of God throughout the world. When God intervenes to rescue a remnant of at least 144,000 faithful Jews, Satan will become enraged and turns his immense anger on the church:

> And the dragon [Satan] *was enraged with the woman* [Israel], *and went off to make war with the rest of her offspring, who keep the commandments of God and hold to the testimony of Jesus....And it was given to him* [the Antichrist] *to make war with the saints and to overcome them; and the authority over every tribe and people and tongue and nation was given to him.* (Revelation 12:17; 13:7).

Apostasy and Betrayal

And at that time many will fall away and will betray one another and hate one another (Matthew 24:10).

Jesus also spoke of apostasy and betrayal. The word

5

apostasy simply means "falling away," and Jesus warned us that because of the pressure from the intense tribulation, many believers would deny their faith. It is one thing to stand in our beautiful auditoriums and sit in plush pews and claim to be Christians. It is something else to risk losing everything, including loved ones and our own life, for that same confession. There are many people in our churches today whose faith has never truly been tested, and during the time of tribulation many of those will fail the test.

But it is worse than that, because many of these people who fall away will be trusted by others in the church. Many who hold steadfast to their confession will discover that some whom they trusted will betray them. That will produce an attitude among believers of mistrust, and as a result, many will become isolated from other believers. Once that happens, they are vulnerable to the enemy.

It is common when a nation is preparing to go to war for it to disseminate information to prepare its citizens, particularly those upon whom it will call to risk their lives in combat. Such a situation often produces a sense of unity throughout the nation so that its citizens have a sense of supporting one another. There is nothing the enemy would like to do more than to provoke disunity and division.

Perhaps it is time that the Body of Christ should begin to prepare.

False Prophets

And many false prophets will arise, and will mislead many (Matthew 24:11).

Another characteristic that Jesus mentions about this time is that there will be a false spiritualism, a supernaturalism that appears to be genuine to the one not trained in the Word of God. As a result, there will be many believers as well as non-believers who will be misled.

In Matthew 24:24 Jesus warned that these false prophets would have the ability to perform "great signs and wonders," so that even the elect are in danger of being misled. Many of us have seen so-called magicians perform acts of illusion, but what happens with the Antichrist in this time will be very real. In this time there will be one who will assist the Antichrist:

> *And he performs great signs, so that he even makes fire come down out of heaven to the earth in the presence of men. And he deceives those who dwell on the earth because of the signs which it was given him to perform in the presence of the beast* [Antichrist] (Revelation 13:13-14).

With our satellite communications today, even a small group of wonder-workers can be known worldwide and generate a tremendous amount of support.

Being a Christian is no guarantee that we will be safe from this deception. Jesus warned that even some, perhaps many, believers will be deceived (Matthew 24:24).

Lawlessness

And because lawlessness is increased...

One of the ways in which a person can gain great political power is to create a situation where the normal moral fiber of society is torn and destroyed. When the

7

normal order of law breaks down and the external societal restraints are removed, normally law abiding people often become criminals looting and stealing, even if it means hurting those around them. Their love and respect for one another, the glue that holds societies together, fades as the external structure disappears.

This can be often seen in mob riots, but one of the best examples was Germany in the 1920s and 1930s. Germany's loss in World War I in 1918 and the subsequent punitive actions of the victorious allies devastated Germany's economy, creating great hardship. Into this situation stepped Adolf Hitler, who was the head of a small radical and violent political party. His strategy was to create great chaos into which he would step and bring order.

It is going to take great personal integrity and endurance to survive in such a situation without succumbing to the mob atmosphere.

Lawlessness in the Church

Most people's love will grow cold (Matthew 24:12).

Jesus' use of the word "love" in Matthew 24:12 gives an added dimension to His warning. The word "love" used here is the word agape in the Greek. As used by Jesus in this case, *agape* refers to either the believer's love of God, or as in John 13:35, the love of believers for one another. In Revelation 2:4 Jesus warned the church in Ephesus that they had left their "first love." During His final celebration of the Passover with His disciples, Jesus told them that "if you love Me, you will keep My commandments" (John 14:15).

From this it can be inferred that Jesus is specifically

talking of and to the Church. He is warning of lawlessness, by which Jesus means rebellion against authority.

Lawlessness in the church is not living in obedient submission to Jesus as Lord. The persecuted church must learn to walk in humble obedience to God and to His appointed men of authority. The writer of Hebrews states, "Obey your leaders, and submit to them." (Hebrews 13:17)

Preaching of the Gospel

And this gospel of the kingdom shall be preached in the whole world for a witness to all the nations, and then the end shall come (Matthew 24:14).

Finally Jesus said the Gospel of the kingdom would be preached to the whole world. In recent years the evangelical church has had a strong sense of evangelism, and among evangelical churches today there is often a sense of urgency to go into all the world to preach the Gospel. This desire is good and healthy, but Jesus is not waiting for us to reach all of the world with the Gospel before He initiates the events that lead to His return.

Jesus' statement here that the Gospel would be preached to the whole world is said in the context of a persecuted church suffering tribulation. It is hard to imagine the church suffering such persecution and, at the same time, doing world-wide evangelism. Thus, this is not evangelism as we know it today, but most likely a supernatural preaching of which everyone in the world would be aware.

One possibility as to how this would occur is given in Revelation 11 where the two witnesses declare the word of the Lord to the entire world. These two men testify supernaturally to the whole world during this time of tribulation.

The Return of Jesus

Jesus promised His followers, "the elect," that for their sake He would not allow the tribulation to run its full course. So far, Satan has had his way with the tribulation, and if he were allowed to continue, he might be successful in eliminating the faithful from the face of the earth. But on a day and at a time that no one knows Jesus says, "Enough is enough."

The Day of the Lord

But immediately after the tribulation of those days the sun will be darkened, and the moon will not give its light, and the stars will fall from the sky, and the powers of the heavens will be shaken, and then the sign of the Son of Man will appear in the sky, and then all the tribes of the earth will mourn, and they will see the Son of Man coming on the clouds of the sky with power and great glory (Matthew 24:29-30).

At this point in the narrative, Jesus turned to the Old Testament prophets to provide the description of what it will be like when He says, "Enough!" There are going to be signs in the heavens: the sun will turn dark, the moon also will not give its light, and the stars will fall from the sky. These are the same types of signs that the prophets said would herald the day of the Lord (See, for example, Joel 2:30-31).

Then the "sign of the Son of Man" will appear everywhere over the earth, so that all men everywhere will see it together. It will appear suddenly, like lightning flashing from the east to the west.

More importantly, these would also be signs for the believers who are still remaining. It is easy to imagine that after years of being hunted and killed, the remaining saints will be discouraged. For most of them they will probably be in hiding, surviving in whatever way they can. Suddenly they will look up and see supernatural signs in the heavens and know that Jesus is on His way to rescue them. No longer will they have to slink around like hunted animals, but they will be able to stand up straight, proud that they have remained faithful and rejoicing that they will soon see Jesus. As Luke states it, "When you see these things begin to take place, straighten up and lift up your heads, because your redemption is drawing near" (Luke 21:28).

The Rapture

But the one who endures to the end, it is he who shall be saved....And He will send forth His angels with a great trumpet and they will gather together His elect from the four winds, from one end of the sky to the other (Matthew 24:13, 31).

The Day of the Lord is when Jesus will come to bring God's wrath and judgment on Satan. But before He begins, He must remove the remaining faithful believers, "the elect," so that they will not experience the wrath of God. So He will send forth His angels to gather them together and bring them to Himself. This is what is often called the "rapture," or catching up, of the church. Marvin Rosenthal calls this the "pre-wrath rapture of the church."[2]

It is quite sobering to read Jesus' answer to the disciples question, and it should give us reason to stop and think. If the rapture of the church occurs prior to the tribulation, then there is no need for Jesus to give such warnings. If believers will not go through a time of great testing, then why would Jesus say to us, "The one who endures to the end, it is he who will be saved"?

The rapture is not a time of escape, but a time of great victory. Concerning this time, Luke records Jesus as saying,

> *But when these things begin to take place, straighten up and lift up your heads, because your redemption is drawing near* (Luke 21:28).

Jesus has a reason for telling us these things, and it is so that we may be warned beforehand. "Behold," He says, "I have told you in advance." (Matthew 24:25)[3]

CHAPTER NOTES

[1] Krus, David J. and Blackman, Harold S., "Time-Scale Factor as Related to Theories of Societal Change," *Psychological Reports*, 1980, No. 46, pp. 95-102.

[2] Rosenthal, Marvin, *The Pre-Wrath Rapture of the Church,* Thomas Nelson Publishers, Nashville, 1990.

[3] For a detailed examination of prophetic scriptures, see *The Coming Day of the Lord: Understanding the Prophecies About the Return of Jesus*, by Daniel M. Sweger.

CHAPTER 2

Blessing and Purification

Count it all joy, my brethren, when you encounter
various trials (James 1:2).

After World War II Mennonite missionaries were active in Ethiopia, and one of the results of their efforts was the start of the *Meserete Kristos* (Christ is the Foundation) Church. The first believers were baptized in 1952, and the church continued to grow. Eventually the missionaries handed the administration of the church over to the Ethiopians.

In 1974 a Marxist government took power in the country, and in 1982 the government outlawed the church. At that time they had 5000 members, and the government seized all their properties and closed the church. The leaders were imprisoned and most of the missionaries left the country. It was a time of intense fear.

At the celebration of their 50th anniversary in 2002, Kassa Agafari, the pastoral secretary of Meserete Kristos, recalled that time. "When the church was closed and the missionaries left, we felt like the Israelites when the ark was captured by the Philistines—Ichabod—the glory has departed. We wondered if MKC would die."

Kassa Agafari continued: "When the church was closed, only those who had died to self came to us. They didn't fear for their lives. They were like grains of wheat

13

in the ground. God purified us and gave us new vision and zeal."

Religious freedom was restored in 1991 after the Marxists were ousted. When the believers again assembled, Meserete Kristos discovered that they numbered 50,000! They had grown ten-fold in the nine years of persecution. By the time of their jubilee celebration, the church had 264 congregations, 584 church planting centers, a faith community of 178,622 people throughout the nation, and over 88,000 baptized believers.[1]

Tribulation and Blessing

There is a belief among Christians in the United States and Europe that it is almost their right not to suffer real tribulation. Tribulation comes at the hands of governments, and few Christians have suffered real persecution in Western democracies for hundreds of years. Yet in many countries of the world, Christians are subjected daily to tribulation for their belief. Furthermore, Jesus made it plain that we will be blessed when we do suffer persecution for His name's sake (Matthew 5:11-12).

It has become a popular teaching that the church will be removed from the earth prior to all of what Jesus warned His disciples would happen. This false teaching would have us believe that we will not suffer under the one we call the Antichrist. However, one can make the case that if believers were not to suffer tribulation under the Antichrist, there would be no need for Jesus to make such a major issue of this in Matthew 24:15-21.

Those who teach that the church will be removed prior to these events do so because they know that believers will never experience the wrath and judgment of

God. It is true that as believers we have been saved and delivered from God's judgment, and as such we will never experience His wrath.

It is important to understand, however, that the tribulation spoken of by Jesus here is not God's wrath. According to Revelation 12:13, the tribulation is the wrath of Satan and not the wrath of God. This point cannot be overstressed. As recorded in the Sermon on the Mount, Jesus taught His followers that it is a blessing to experience the wrath of Satan in the form of persecution. Tribulation and trials in the life of the believer are not God's punishment, but rather His blessing.

I recently came upon a fascinating quotation by Dennis Balcombe as he was visiting brothers and sisters in Christ in China.

> [A brother in China] stood up in the meeting and began to share about what had happened in prison. Everyone began to weep and I at first thought they felt bad for the suffering he had to endure. Then I heard people saying, "Lord, how blessed he is that he can suffer for you. Oh, that You would allow me the same privilege." I realized they were all envious of this believer, for he was especially chosen of the Lord for this honour.[2]

What a different attitude than the typical western Christian! It is part of our lifestyle that we, as saints, are to have joy. It is one of the fruits of living in the spirit. However, there is a special joy for those who are faithful in tribulation. It is like the joy that an athlete, who has been tested to the limit of his endurance and wins, has as he stands on the podium and receives the gold medal. That is why James could write to the believers, "Count it all joy, my brethren, when you encounter various trials, knowing that the testing of your faith produces endurance."

Tribulation and Purification

Much of the Old Testament is a record of how Israel was unfaithful to God, and how God occasionally allowed Israel's enemies to defeat her in order to purify her and bring her back to Himself. When things had deteriorated so far that there seemed to be no returning, God allowed the Babylonians under Nebuchadnezzar to destroy Jerusalem and deport the people to Babylon. God used godless people to purify His people.

It is going to be the same with the Church. The Bible testifies that the Church is being prepared as a bride for Jesus. In Ephesians Paul writes that Jesus is going to present Himself with a bride.

> *That He might present to Himself the church in all her glory, have no spot or wrinkle or any such thing; but that she should be holy and blameless* (Ephesians 5:27).

There are few today who would argue that the church in America or anywhere else is pure and blameless. We often look the other way at sin and excuse immoral behavior, even in church leaders. Yet Peter indicates that judgment begins "with the household of God" (I Peter 4:17). The church must undergo a process of purification. The image that the Bible uses to communicate what this process is like is that of the metallurgist who is refining silver. Concerning Israel God says,

> *But who can endure the day of His coming? And who can stand when He appears? For He is like a re-*

16

*finer's fire and like fullers' soap. He will sit as a
smelter and purifier of silver, and He will purify the
sons of Levi and refine them like gold and silver, so
that they may present to the Lord offerings in righteousness* (Malachi 3:2-3).

Speaking also of the day of the Lord, Zechariah
states,

*"It will come about in all the land," declares the
Lord, "that two parts of it will be cut off and perish;
But the third will be left in it. "And I will bring the
third part through the fire, Refine them as silver is
refined, And test them as gold is tested. They will call
on My name, And I will answer them; I will say,
'They are My people,'And they will say, 'The Lord is
my God'"* (Zechariah 13:8-9).

What is true for Israel is also true for the church. As
Titus writes,

*For the grace of God has appeared, bringing salva-
tion to all men, instructing us to deny ungodliness
and worldly desires and to live sensibly, righteously
and godly in the present age, looking for the blessed
hope and the appearing of the glory of our great God
and Savior, Christ Jesus; who gave Himself for us,
that He might redeem us from every lawless deed
and* purify for Himself a people *for His own possession, zealous for good deeds* (Titus 2:11-14, emphasis
added).

In the description of the Marriage of the Lamb in
Revelation 19, the bride is described as being clothed
"in fine linen, bright and clean" (v.8). As Malachi speaks
of the "fullers' soap," the church must go through a
process of purification similar to Israel.

The process of refining silver and gold is a long and exacting one. First, the ore is placed in a crucible and heated white hot. As the ore melts, the more dense metal sinks to the bottom and the impurities, also called dross, float to the surface. The refiner carefully and skillfully skims the impurities from the surface so as not to remove any of the metal. He then makes the fire a little hotter, and more impurities float to the surface so that he can skim them too. After doing this several times, each time increasing the temperature of the fire, there are no more impurities, and the surface of the metal looks like a mirror, perfectly reflecting the image of the refiner as he looks at it.

In terms of the Church and the children of Israel, the refining fire is persecution and tribulation. Although much of the church worldwide lives under the threat of persecution, the church in the United States and much of the western world has known little of persecution. Although a large percentage of the adult population in the U.S. claims to be born again, it is virtually impossible to know how strong the church really is. As the heat of persecution and tribulation gets turned up, many are going to fall away, submitting to the demands of the Antichrist and betraying believers. This is what Paul called the apostasy. It is also the dross floating to the surface.

One of the criticisms that unbelievers often have of Christians is that they are hypocrites. While this is sometimes just an excuse on their part, it is often difficult to see much difference between the world and the church in the behavior of believers. The word "Christian" means "like Christ," but that image is often badly distorted to the world.

As the tribulation increases, the church will become more pure until it finally reflects accurately the face of the Refiner. The great tribulation spoken of by Jesus is not His wrath, rather it is a time of separating the pure metal from the dross, the wheat from the chaff.

Surely as things stand now the Bride of Christ's garments are not "bright and clean." The people of God, both in the church and Israel, must undergo a purifying process before they are ready to receive their King. And it is the Antichrist that God uses to do that.

CHAPTER NOTES

[1] African Christianity: A History of the Christian Church in Africa, "Ethiopian Protestantism: The "Pente" Churches in Ethiopia, "http://www.bethel.edu/~letnie/AfricanChristianity/EthiopiaProtestantism.html.
Eastern Mennoite Missions—Explore Resources, "Meserete Kristos Church celebrates Jubilee," http://www.emm.org/resources/article.cfm?articleID=31

[2] Virgo, Terry, *Start*, Kingsway Publications (Eastbourne, UK) 1988, p. 178.

CHAPTER 3

Understanding the Times

Now learn the parable from the fig tree... (Luke 21:36)

I t is perhaps a stereotypical scene: The car is loaded with all the paraphernalia for the vacation, and the entire family is excited as they drive towards grandma and grandpa's house. It is a long, long drive, and the children can't wait to get there. Before long a plaintiff cry comes from the back seat, "Are we there yet?" After asking this several times and getting the same answer ("It's still a long, long way."), the children settle down for the long wait.

We used to play games with the kids, or read, or nap in order to pass the time. Even so, it always seemed that we would never arrive until all of a sudden someone spotted a familiar landmark. Then everyone knew that we were almost there!

One almost gets a picture of the disciples asking Jesus, "Is it time yet? How long are we going to have to wait?" Jesus' answer is, in effect, "It is still a long, long way" (Acts 1:6,7). How are we going to know when it is almost time?

There seems to be a growing expectation that we are quickly approaching the time of His return. Many in the Church are declaring that Jesus is coming soon. While this is an exciting prospect, many have declared His coming in the past and have been wrong. Is there some objective measure we can use?

The answer to that question is "Yes." Jesus gave us a specific landmark, a sign post, so that when we see it we would know that the time is near.

The Parable of the Fig Tree

Now learn the parable from the fig tree: when its branch has already become tender, and puts forth its leaves, you know that summer is near; even so you too, when you see all these things, recognize that He is near, right at the door (Matthew 24:32-33)

Figs in Israel of Jesus' day were considered to be a delicacy, and there were two types of fig trees. The more prized tree, the black and white *boccore*, or early fig, produced its fruit in the spring before the leaves appeared on the tree.[1] The leaves appeared so late in the spring that they were considered to be the final sign that the hot, dry summer was beginning.

However, there is more to this parable than this. What Jesus said in this passage is not complete, which is why He told us to "learn the parable." Actually what He said here is the conclusion of the parable. It begins in Luke.

And He began telling them this parable: "A certain man had a fig tree which had been planted in his vineyard; and he came looking for fruit on it, and did not find any. And he said to the vineyardkeeper, 'Behold, for three years I have come looking for fruit on this fig tree without finding any. Cut it down! Why does it even use up the ground?' And he answered and said to him, 'Let it alone, sir, for this

21

year too, until I did around it and put in fertilizer; and if it bears fruit next year, fine; but if not, cut it down"' (Luke 13:6-9).

In this parable Jesus was speaking of the nation of Israel. The emphasis here is on the figs, or the fruitfulness of the nation with respect to Himself. He is speaking about the fruit of repentance that John the Baptist had so often called for, and so far the nation had yet to repent of its selfish ways and receive her Messiah.

At the time Jesus spoke this parable, it had been more than two years since His baptism by John inaugurated His public ministry. Each year He would go up to Jerusalem for the Feast of the Passover, and during the course of His three and a half years of ministry, He went to the feast four times. So far He had been to Jerusalem three times, and three times the priests and Pharisees had rejected Him.

Jesus was the one speaking in this parable, and He told the vineyard man (possibly Michael, the archangel who watches over Israel) to destroy Israel since it was fruitless. The vineyard man in turn pleaded with Jesus to give him one more year. He promised to do what every good gardener does and see if he could not get it to bear fruit. So Jesus gave him one more year.

But this is not the end of the parable, because there is yet one more year. The next time Jesus went up to Jerusalem for the Passover was His last time. Several days before the feast began, He rode into the city on a donkey, which is a direct fulfillment of prophecy (Zechariah 9:9). By doing this He openly declared to the entire nation that He was their Messiah, and yet they rejected Him again.

The very next day Jesus entered the city early in the morning.[2] The previous night was probably spent at the house of Lazarus in Bethany, and thus He would have approached the city from the east. As he approached the city he saw a fig tree in full leaf, and He went over to it. Seeing no fruit, He cursed it, saying, "No longer shall there ever be any fruit from you." It is recorded that the fig tree withered and died at once. In the Mark account the disciples remarked that the tree had "withered from the roots up."

This is a strange incident. It would almost seem that Jesus, in a fit of anger totally uncharacteristic of Him, cursed the tree. Jesus had a right to expect to find fruit, and yet there was none. What He did by cursing the tree only makes sense if it is an extension of the parable recorded by Luke. Instead of relating the parable using words, however, Jesus acted it out.

This method of telling a parable, i.e. by acting rather than speaking, is not unusual in the Bible. For example, the prophet Jeremiah did it on several occasions, as did Hosea. When Jesus approached the fig tree, it was not so much that He did not find figs on it as that tree was symbolic of the fact that there was still no fruit in Israel. Just the previous day, the leaders rejected Jesus as they had done for the previous three times He had come to Jerusalem for the feast. Like the vineyardkeeper of the parable in Luke, He had it cut down when He cursed it.

History, of course, proves out what had happened. Within a few years the Temple was destroyed, and Israel died as a nation.

The final part of this parable takes place on the Mount of Olives as Jesus tells us to "learn the parable from the fig tree." It is important to understand that this is the same fig tree that had no fruit in the parable recorded in Luke and the one that was cursed by Jesus so that it died. Notice, however, that the fig tree is no longer dead, but is putting forth its leaves.

There are two things to note in this context. The first is that the only way a dead tree can put forth leaves is that it is supernaturally revived. It is not possible in the natural understanding of the way in which things operate to explain how this once dead tree can put forth leaves. Secondly, there is no mention of fruit on the tree. It is as if the fruitfulness of the nation is no longer an issue.

This is the parable of the fig tree: The nation of Israel, who was cursed and died because it rejected the One sent to it as its Messiah, will come to life again. It will, as it were, be resurrected. It will come to life again in a supernatural way, but will still not recognize its Messiah.

Finally, when we see these things happen, we are to know that the time is close. Jesus went on to mention that "this generation will not pass away until all these things take place" (Matthew 24:34).

Israel—the Sign Post

Many of the prophecies surrounding the return of Jesus and the fulfillment of God's promises to the Jews do not make sense unless there is a strong, independent nation of Israel. On May 14, 1948 an event unlike any other in the history of the world occurred. By a declaration of an international body of nations a piece of land was declared a nation. Is this nation, which we call Israel, the fig tree that Jesus spoke of?

The Bible, and the Old Testament in particular, abounds with prophecies concerning the restoration of Israel. In addition, most of these prophecies are closely tied to the end times and the appearance of the Messiah.

So the first question that must be answered in order to determine whether the present day Israel is the same as the Israel of end time prophecy is, does this nation fulfill prophecy?

The prophet Ezekiel spoke much about the restoration of Israel. Some of these prophetic statements are listed below:

- God will gather the people from the countries (28:25-26).
- God will be like a shepherd to them and supernaturally restore the land (34:11-31).
- The land has become desolate and a possession of many nations (a powerful prophecy) (36:4).
- God will restore it before the nations (36:9-10,34).
- God is not doing this for Israel's sake, but for His holy name (36:22).
- Israel and Judah will become one (37:15-23).

Isaiah also spoke of the restored nation.
- A nation will be born in one day. (66:8)
- The people will be called from the four corners of the world (Isaiah 43:5-7).

Two things stand out from these scriptures. First, the present nation of Israel satisfies all of these prophecies; and secondly, God only spoke of one restoration, and that in the context of the day of the Lord. One can only conclude that Israel today is the fig tree spoken of by Jesus. It has come to life and put forth its leaves.

Some have tried to use the statement of Jesus that "this generation shall not pass away" to determine the time at which Jesus will return. One wildly popular idea was that the time of a generation was 40 years, and since Israel become a nation in 1948, He would come in

1988. That obviously was incorrect, but that does not diminish Jesus' statement. The generation that saw the founding of Israel is still here, but that will not last forever. One cannot help coming to the conclusion that Jesus is indeed right at the door.

Understanding the Times

Luke recorded some of Jesus' teachings concerning His return in Luke 12:35-58. Most of the time that Jesus talked of these things He spoke privately to the disciples, but there is one instance in particular when He turned to the crowd.

> *And He was also saying to the multitudes, "When you see a cloud rising in the west, immediately you say, 'A shower is coming,' and so it turns out. And when you see a south wind blowing, you say, 'It will be a hot day,' and it turns out that way. You hypocrites! You know how to analyze the appearance of the earth and the sky, but why do you not analyze this present time?"* (Luke 12:54-56)

In typical fashion, Jesus used illustrations of things with which everyone was familiar. Most of the people were directly concerned with agriculture, and so He knew the weather was important to them. Today, He might say, "You know how to take polls to find out what is happening in politics," or "You know how to analyze a corporate balance sheet." We know how to talk about the things that affect and concern us on a daily basis.

There is nothing wrong with that, yet He called the people "hypocrites." That word was one of the strongest rebukes He ever used. The reason was that the people put a higher priority on recognizing weather patterns than they did on understanding and applying biblical prophecy to the time in which they lived. Jesus was standing in front of them, a living, breathing fulfillment of prophecy, and they totally missed it.

Today we also have a living fulfillment of prophecy that is in the headlines of the news virtually every day. The nation of Israel and what is happening in the Middle East is not accidental. How can we remain ignorant?

It has been a long time since Jesus ascended back to His Father. In fact, it has been so long that it is difficult to imagine that the wait is almost over. I believe that for those who are asking, "Are we there yet?" God is answering, "Almost. Just look for the signs."

CHAPTER NOTES

[1] *International Bible Dictionary*, Logos International (Plainfield, NJ), 1977, p. 153.

[2] The incident of the fig tree is recorded in Matthew 21:18-22; Mark 11:12-14, 20-24.

CHAPTER 4

Get Ready!

But keep on the alert at all times... (Luke 21:36)

On September 11, 2001, the economic center of the United States was attacked when two fully loaded commercial jet airliners crashed into the twin towers of the World Trade Center in New York City. A short time later, the military center of the United States was attacked when another airliner was crashed into the Pentagon. Yet a fourth airliner was flown into the ground in rural Pennsylvania as the crew and passengers overwhelmed the agents who had hijacked the airplane. That airplane was apparently targeted to attack the White House, the political center of the United States. That day millions of stunned Americans stared at their television screens, listened to their radios, or logged into the internet, mesmerized and shocked by what they saw and heard.

The impact of those singular attacks have been more far reaching that the simple magnitude of the attacks would warrant. Fewer than 3,000 people were killed, which is less than 10% of those killed in automobile accidents each year. The site of the Twin Towers has been cleaned up and the damage to the Pentagon has been repaired. Yet the United States remains a shaken nation.

For more than 10 years, since the collapse of the

Soviet Union, the United States arguably was the only super power left among the nations of the world. It has also been identified by the world as one of the most Christianized nations of the world. How could such a thing happen?

The United States was totally unprepared for the events of that day. The military and government at all levels were caught sleeping. Even the powerful secret intelligence agencies responsible for warning of such events were clueless. Given that situation, it is quite understandable that the citizenry was so shaken.

Were there no clues? Of course there were. Were there no signs? Of course there were, but for years those in responsible positions were either unable to read them and discern what they meant, or they ignored them.

Is it possible that God is using such an event to alert the church to her present situation? Would God be so cruel as to know that the horrific events of the tribulation were going to occur and yet not provide a warning for His people? God is merciful, and He gives us instructions on how we can be prepared for the events to come.

When Paul wrote to Timothy, his son in the Lord, he used the illustration that we are like soldiers of Jesus (II Timothy 2:3-4). When soldiers go through boot camp, they go through a process of intense training in two major areas.

First, they are taught the principles and skills they need as individuals. They learn how to use and care for their weapons; they become physically fit and strong; they learn how to do battle.

Then they are taught how to function together as a unit. If an army is going to be effective in battle, the soldiers must learn how to function together and have cohesion. They learn the chain of command so they know whom to obey. Individuals are put together in small groups that soon function as a unit. Each one is assigned a specific job and learn the skills to accomplish that job effectively.

It is the same way in the Church. We must learn what to do both individually and corporately. The rest of the book is divided into two main sections to reflect these needs.

Being Wise

After Jesus had finished answering the disciples' questions on the sign of His return, He went on to give them some instruction. As was His usual method of teaching, He told them a series of parables. These parables take up about 2/3 of the Olivet Discourse, as found in Matthew 24 and 25, and can be approached from many perspectives. The context in which Jesus told these parables, however, is prophetic and they were given for the benefit of believers facing the times and trials that Jesus had just spoken about.

These parables are:
- The Days of Noah
- The Parable of the Thief
- The Parable of the Wise and Evil Slaves
- The Parable of the Ten Virgins
- The Parable of the Talents
- The Parable of the Sheep and Goats

The next section, consisting of Chapters 5-11, will look at each of these parables from the perspective of what we need to be doing, as believers, to prepare.

Getting the Church Ready

It is not sufficient for believers to be equipped unless they are also joined together with other believers. Jesus would not be so inconsiderate so as to leave the church without solutions in the coming crisis.

In the first chapter of Revelation, Jesus appears to John and tells him to write down letters for seven churches in the Roman province of Asia (present day western Turkey). Jesus then proceeds to dictate these letters to John.

To understand these letters it is important to note that the entire book of Revelation is addressed to "the seven churches that are in Asia." Since the rest of the book is clearly prophetic, outlining in great detail the events to come, it is fair to consider that these letters, written to actual churches in that day, are also prophetic.

In these letters Jesus is giving instruction to the end-time church. The situations with the seven churches in Asia are the same as the situations that are being faced by churches all over the world as we approach the end times.

CHAPTER 5

Acting in Faith

For the coming of the Son of Man will be just like the days of Noah (Matthew 24:37).

Noah had awakened early that morning, and as he walked out of his house a heavy mist hung over everything. It was an ideal place to live. Artesian springs of warm water flowed over the land, and although there was not much difference in temperature between day and night, the slight cooling at night caused a heavy fog to settle over everything. This fog watered the abundant vegetation, making the whole earth like a beautiful garden.

Yet in the midst of this beauty was violence and wickedness. Noah was now 500 years old, and in his lifetime he had watched brutality and cruelty increase around him. It almost seemed that he was alone, almost a stranger in this world because of his love and devotion to God.

His heart was heavy as he pondered what Yahweh had told him the day before. God was about to destroy life on this magnificent planet that He had created especially for man. He said He was going to send an enormous flood of water that would cover the entire earth and destroy all mankind.

As Noah found his way to one of the warm springs to

wash his face, he wondered about those things God had told him. He had never even seen any kind of a storm, yet God had told him to build an enormous box, an ark He called it, so that he and his family would be safe from this flood. He headed back home to talk to his family and start the preparations for the enormous task ahead.

Noah's Faith

For the coming of the Son of Man will be just like the days of Noah. For as in those days which were before the flood they were eating and drinking, they were marrying and giving in marriage, until the day that Noah entered the ark, and they did not understand until the flood came and took them all away, so shall the coming of the Son of Man be (Matthew 24:37-39).

The first impression that one gets reading this passage is that there is not going to be any warning of Christ's return until that day. Life simply goes on as usual, and we are all clueless as to what is going to happen. Then Jesus suddenly comes bringing judgment.

To make that assumption, however, is to be ignorant of what the days of Noah were like and what Noah did. In fact, the people of Noah's day were not ignorant of what was coming. Rather they chose to ignore the warnings.

Noah Delivered God's Warning to the World

When God first spoke to Noah and announced His intention of bringing judgment on the earth, Noah was 500 years old. For more than 100 years, Noah and his family worked on the ark, a visible testimony to the entire world. Moreover, Peter testified that Noah was "a preacher of righteousness" (II Peter 2:5), proclaiming to the world by the words he spoke and the actions he performed what was about to happen. The result was that no one was without excuse. Noah was like a watchman on the wall of the fortress, proclaiming impending danger.

God spoke a prophetic word through the prophet Ezekiel that He would raise up watchmen on the wall of the city (Ezekiel 33:1-9). The job of the watchman was to stand on the wall of the city and look in the distance for the enemy's approach. When he saw the army of the enemy approaching, the watchman was to sound the alarm by blowing on the trumpet. It was then the responsibility of those within the city to respond to the warning. If, however, the watchman failed to sound the alarm then the full responsibility for the resulting loss of life fell on his shoulders.

In a like manner, God is raising up men and women who are alert to both the biblical prophetic warnings and the signs of the times to be watchmen on the wall. It is their job to announce to the church the times and seasons, particularly as the judgment approaches. If they fail to do their job then many in the body of Christ will perish needlessly, and that responsibility will be theirs.

Method of Judgment Did Not Fit Their Paradigm

The record of Genesis indicates that violent weather, such as high winds and strong storms, was unknown in the years prior to the Great Flood.[1] The climate of the earth was particularly well suited for life, so that people lived exceptionally long lives by our standards. It was therefore difficult for the people to imagine what Noah was talking about when he spoke of a flood or what was the purpose of the ark.

One of the difficult things with which Christians and non-Christians alike struggle is the description of what things are going to be like on earth during the days leading up to the return of Jesus. It is outside the realm of our experience for there to be such control over the nations and peoples of the world by one man.

We have been taught that the world will continue on in its present state for many years to come. Evolution is the dominant world-view in society today. In that framework of thought, global changes, if they occur at all, take millions of years to be noticed, and anyone who announces the end of the world is considered by most to be on the fringes of reality.

The apostle Peter encountered this same basic mode of thinking, and he must have been thinking of Jesus' words when he wrote,

> *Know this first of all, that in the last days mockers will come with there mocking, following after their own lusts, and saying, "Where is the promise of His coming? For ever since the fathers fell asleep, all continues just as it was from the beginning of creation." For when they maintain this, it escapes their notice that by the word of God the heavens existed long ago and the earth was formed out of water and by water, through which the world at that time was destroyed, being flooded with water. But the present heavens and earth by His word are being reserved for fire, kept for the day of judgment and destruction of ungodly men* (II Peter 3:3-7).

Noah Responded to God in Faith

In Hebrews 11, known as the Hall of Faith, Noah is

listed as one of the "men of old" who responded in faith to the word of God. Noah had no more of an idea of the magnitude of what was going to happen than anyone else. Everything seemed to be going on as usual, but behind the scenes God was preparing. It was in response to God's word to him, not the circumstances that he observed, that Noah began to make preparations. He responded in faith, not yet seeing the substance of what God had spoken. Because of his preparations, he was able to take others with him—his wife and family.

Everyone who heard Noah testify, and that encompassed the entire world, had a decision to make. Note that the door of the ark was not closed until judgment started, and only then it was too late. Until that time anyone could have gotten on the ark and been safe, but they all chose to ignore the warnings of Noah. It is estimated that the population of the world at that time was at least 1.5 billion people, yet how tragic it is that not one single person responded in faith.

Our Faith

There is certainly a sense in which believers should be prepared at all times. However, like He did with Noah, God is giving specific warnings to believers to get ready. God is raising up prophetic voices announcing impending judgment all over the globe. He is telling us to get ready.

The chorus of prophetic voices is growing, and yet, by and large, it is making little change in how we live and prepare. If we continue to hear the word of God and yet make no changes in our lifestyle, we may be unprepared for what is about to happen.

Perhaps we have such a difficult time acting in accordance with the warning because such an idea of the end of the world is too outlandish. It is so far outside of our day to day experience that it is beyond our comprehension. It is easier to ignore the warnings than it is to change our ideas.

Are we afraid of criticism and ridicule? What happens if we are wrong? Won't we seem like fools? These are serious questions that need to be answered. Paul wrote that "God was well-pleased through the foolishness of the message preached to save those who believe" (I Corinthians 1:21).

Faith is more than mental assent. It has to be expressed in actions. Perhaps we need to talk about these things and make some plans. Our plans should include provision for taking as many to safety as possible.

God did not build the ark; Noah did. Without the ark Noah would have perished along with the rest of mankind. Like Noah, there are going to be many who do not understand and will challenge us. But some will understand and respond to the word of God.

CHAPTER NOTES

[1] There are many excellent books on the subject of the pre-Flood world. One of the best is *The Biblical Basis for Modern Science* by Henry Morris.

CHAPTER 6

Awake and Ready

Therefore, be on the alert (Matthew 24:42).

A few years ago there was great concern as the year 2000 approached. It was an interesting time as many forecasters were predicting a great catastrophe because computers around the world would misinterpret the date. Known as the "Y2K crisis," it occurred because most computer programmers used an abbreviated form of the year in dates. As a software developer myself, I spent a lot of time converting my software to handle that situation.

Nobody knew for sure what was going to happen, even in the heart of Africa. In a conversation I recently had with a good friend in Zambia, he reported that even the people in the villages were instructed to gather extra firewood. The questions on most peoples' lips were, "What is going to happen, and what can we do?" Some people did nothing, preferring to take their chances. Many, including myself, began making some sort of preparations. Others seemed to go to extremes. Not wanting to go to one extreme or the other, we bought a generator (not a bad idea anyway, since we live in a rural area) and stocked up on some food and water.

Being Ready

Therefore be on the alert, for you do not know which day you Lord is coming. But be sure of this, that if the head of the house had known at what time of the night the thief was coming, he would have been on the alert and would have not have allowed his house to be broken into. For this reason you be ready, too (Matthew 24:42-44).

What does it mean for us to be ready for the return of Jesus? Is it like preparing for the Y2K crisis and stockpiling food, or getting a white robe and going out to the nearest mountain top? Is it even possible to be ready?

Many look at this parable and conclude that we, in fact, cannot really know when Jesus is returning. After all, they reason, we cannot know at what time the thief will come. Jesus Himself said that no one would know the day and the hour, so there is really nothing to do.

In this parable, however, Jesus also says that we are to "be on the alert" and "be ready." He must have had something in mind. Moreover, this is not the only time He talked about coming as a thief. In Revelation John records Jesus as saying, "Behold, I am coming like a thief. Blessed is the one who stays awake." (Revelation 16:15)

Jesus is talking about a spiritual condition of being awake and not a physical one, and there are two applications of this principle that are appropriate in this context. One has to do with our physical needs and the other with our spiritual awareness.

Having Treasures

Satan's primary purpose during the tribulation is to entice or deceive as many people as he can into worshiping him. One of the ways in which he can do this is through coercion. This is why he will have the Antichrist institute an economic system whereby anyone seeking to do any financial transaction will have to have an identifying mark. It is also clear from scripture that anyone who takes this mark, and thus submits to the Antichrist, is going be on the receiving end of the wrath of God (Revelation 14:9-11).

The "mark of the beast" has been a much discussed aspect of end-times prophecy, and over the years there have been many attempts to figure out what it will be. It seems that if we can figure out what the mark is then we can avoid taking it. Regardless of what that mark might be, however, the secret to identifying the mark of the beast is to first recognize the beast. It is, after all, his mark.

There is going to be very real pressure put upon us to accept the mark. It seems that anyone who accepts the mark will escape the wrath of Satan. Those who refuse will probably be unable to find even the necessities of life, and some, perhaps many, will die as a result. It will be very difficult for fathers and mothers to see their children suffering, for example, and the pressures to conform will be enormous.

At this time something Jesus taught will take on a new dimension. In Luke's account of the Sermon on the Mount, Jesus said,

> *For this reason I say to you, do not be anxious for your life, as to what you shall eat; nor for your body, as to what you shall put on. For life is more than food, and the body than clothing. ...For all these things the nations of the world eagerly seek; but your Father knows that you need these things. But seek*

His kingdom, and these things shall be added to you.
Do not be afraid, little flock, for your Father has
chosen gladly to give you the kingdom. Sell your pos-
sessions and give to charity; make yourselves purses
which do not wear out, an unfailing treasure in
heaven, where no thief comes near, nor moth de-
stroys. For where your treasure is, there will your
heart be also (Luke 12:22, 30-34).

Everyone is going to be put in a position where they are going to have to choose. If we have been living a life-style where success and self-worth are measured in material things, then we are going to face overwhelming pressures, whether we are Christian or not.

One of the ways in which we prepare is to adopt a lifestyle that releases us from the bondage of things. Many of us are highly dependent on nice clothes, expensive houses, and an abundance of food. But Jesus said that we can use our present abundance to lay up treasures in heaven. Perhaps that is the type of preparation He has in mind.

We can find ways in which to break the hold of material things in our lives. Jesus speaks of selling our possessions and giving to charity. Perhaps there is something of particular value to us with which we feel that we simply cannot part. The intrinsic value of an item may be much or little, but if we cannot part with it, then its value to us is too high.

Several years ago the guest speaker at our church's annual missions conference was Harold Caballeros from Guatemala. On the first night of the conference he felt impressed to call us to have what he called a "hurting offering." His suggestion was that we identify something that was so valuable to us that it, or what it represented, stood between God and ourselves. We would then make that thing an offering on Sunday morning.

That Sunday morning there was a high degree of expectancy during the service. It was like people were sitting on the edge of their seats waiting for the opportunity to see what God was going to do. When Harold finally gave the invitation, hundreds of people streamed forward. The altar rail filled with computers, money, tools, sporting equipment, jewelry, and other things. Some people wept as they left their items behind.

Then people began to give testimony about what God was doing. They spoke of freedom and release. One woman, a struggling single mother of two children, testified how God told her to empty her bank account and bring it all to the altar. She humbly wept the entire time she was speaking, but before she had a chance to return to her seat people began coming forward and giving her money. There was so much she could not hold it, so those standing by emptied tissue boxes and filled them with the bills. She returned to her seat with two tissue boxes filled to overflowing. Later, she gave one of them to another single mother in a similar situation.

What victory that morning! We got a glimpse of what Jesus meant when He said, "And how do you benefit if you gain the whole world but lose or forfeit your own soul in the process?" (Luke 9:25)

Being Awake

Jonah was a prophet of God who received a call to go to the city of Nineveh. Nineveh was a great city located between the Tigris and Euphrates Rivers in what is now northern Iraq. It had fallen into sin and idolatry, and God called Jonah to prophesy to the people and warn them of God's impending judgment. Jonah had no love for the people of Nineveh and did not really want to see them repent. So instead of obeying God and going eastward toward Nineveh, he boarded a ship bound for Tarshish, far to the west. It was not long before the ship encountered a ferocious storm that threatened to break up the ship. The crew recognized that the storm was of supernatural origin and attempted to test each person aboard as to why God would be so angry. When Jonah was not among them, they sought him out and found him deep in the middle of the ship in a sound sleep.

How is it that Jonah could be so asleep in the middle of such a terrible storm? The situation of Jonah sleeping is a metaphor for a common spiritual condition. When we know what the will of God is for us but refuse to do it, we risk falling into a spiritual slumber. We are afraid that if we hear God speaking He will tell us something we do not want to hear, so we close off our spiritual ears.

In such a condition we, like Jonah, become insensitive to the storm gathering around us. Spiritual things are spiritually discerned, and when our spirit is insensitive, we do not understand what is happening. Reality is what is happening in the spiritual realm, not what the newscasters and commentators are saying on our televisions. By the time we may begin to understand what is happening, it will be too late. Here is what Paul said:

> For you yourselves know full well that the day of the Lord will come just like a thief in the night. While they were saying, "Peace and safety!" then destruction will come upon them suddenly like birth pangs upon a woman with child, and they shall not escape (I Thessalonians 5:2-3).

He goes on to say that we "are all sons of light," not

of darkness; "so then let us not sleep as others do, but let us be alert and sober." (v. 6) God neither slumbers or sleeps because He is spirit, and likewise our spirits never sleep as long as we stay in the known will of God.

I want to suggest that there are two things to which we need to pay attention. One is learning to hear God's voice. Prayer is a vital part of each believer's life, provided that we spend time listening to God and not just talking. Someone has suggested that, since we have two ears and only one mouth, we should spend twice as much time listening as talking.

The other thing we need to pay attention to is the study of the word of God, the Bible. This is more than casual reading. It sometimes involves struggling to understand until revelation comes. It is God's written word, and He will give us revelation if we will spend the time and effort. We do not have to be a Bible scholar to understand the Bible. It is the Holy Spirit Who teaches us, not a university professor, and He leads us into all truth.

CHAPTER 7

Responsible Faithfulness

Paul, a bond-servant of Christ Jesus (Romans 1:1).

One evening I was driving home from a meeting at church and was listening to the radio in the car. Being something of a talk-show junkie, I was listening to one that was hosted by Michael Reagan, who is the son of former president of the United States, Ronald Reagan. When I tuned in, he was in the middle of a conversation with a man on the telephone, and it took me a minute to catch up on the conversation.

The caller had apparently been sexually abused as a boy by a clergyman, and Michael was relating that as a young boy he was sexually abused by a trusted counselor at a day-camp. People like that are predators, and their abuse brings about a wound in the victim that is deep and long lasting. Even then, more than 40 years later, Michael still had to deal with the effects that abuse had in his life and relationships.

Who then is the faithful and sensible slave whom his master put in charge of his household to give them their food at the proper time? Blessed is that slave whom his master finds so doing when he comes. Truly I say to you, that he will put him in charge of all his possessions. But if that evil slave says in his heart, "My master is not coming for a long time," and

> *shall begin to beat his fellow-slaves and eat and*
> *drink with drunkards; the master of that slave will*
> *come on a day when he does not expect him and at*
> *an hour which he does not know, and shall cut him*
> *in pieces and assign him a place with the hypocrites;*
> *weeping shall be there and the gnashing of teeth*
> (Matthew 24:45-51).

This particular parable, the parable of the wise and evil slaves, is a difficult one because it speaks directly to our responsibilities, not only to God, but also to other people. In this parable Jesus speaks directly to the problem of abuse in the church and of the punishment that awaits those who are guilty of such abuse. It is not difficult to understand what Jesus is saying, but rather it is hard for us to accept that God would punish believers so harshly.

Slaves

Who then is the faithful and sensible slave...but if
that evil slave...(Matthew 24:45,48).

The setting for this parable is a household where the owner has many slaves. As in any household, there has to be structure in order for it to function properly, and so the owner, i.e. the master of the slaves, selects certain slaves to oversee and provide for the others so that they can do their work.

The word that Jesus used in this parable for slave is the Greek word *doulos*, which is often translated "bond-servant." It is the same word that Paul uses of himself as he introduces himself to the Romans in his letter to them. A bond-servant is not a slave in our conventional understanding, but a person who voluntarily takes that position.

In biblical Hebrew culture, a person could indenture himself to another for a period of time, usually seven years, in order to pay off a debt or gain some favor. Recall how Jacob indentured himself to his uncle in order to gain Rachel in marriage. During this time he had the status of a slave, but when his time was completed he was free to leave.

Occasionally, however, the indentured slave grew to love his master, and life in the master's house was really good. When the time came for him to gain his freedom, he could decide whether life in the house as a slave was better than anything he could get on his own and make his position of slave a permanent one. When this was done, he became a doulos, a bond-servant, and this decision was irreversible.

This is, in fact, the position of the believer in God's household. When Paul writes, "If you confess with your mouth Jesus as Lord, and believe in your heart that God raised Him from the dead, you shall be saved," this is exactly what he is referring to. At the time we say to Jesus, "You are my Lord!" we voluntarily become as a slave to Him. Thus Paul identifies himself as a "bond-servant of Christ Jesus." The most important aspect of being a slave is that you only have one job: to do the will of the master.

Shepherds

In the household of God, Jesus has appointed certain ones to provide for the welfare of others. They are there for our benefit, and God holds them accountable for how they have behaved. With this position of authority comes the responsibility to take proper care of those under their charge. The writer of Hebrews states, "Obey your leaders, and submit to them; for they keep watch over your souls, as those *who will give an account"* (Hebrews 13:17, emphasis added).

The focus of this parable is not on all the slaves, but only on those whom the master has placed in positions of responsibility and oversight. As long as the master is standing there, everyone behaves properly, but when the master leaves, their true nature begins to show. What happens when you think nobody is watching? Do you do what is expected of you or not?

The one group, whom Jesus calls "faithful and sensible," continue to perform their tasks of taking care of the other slaves. When the master returns, he rewards them.

Those in the other group, however, use the absence of the master as an occasion of selfishness, and they begin to abuse the other slaves. Jesus pronounces these evil and says that when He returns, He will bring a terrible judgment upon them.

There is a passage in Ezekiel 34 that is very similar in content to this parable. Here God is speaking against the "shepherds of Israel," for when they were supposed to be feeding the sheep, they were instead feeding themselves.

You eat the fat and clothe yourselves with the wool, you slaughter the fat sheep without feeding the flock. Those who are sickly you have not strengthened, the diseased you have not healed, the broken you have not bound up, the scattered you have not brought back, nor have you sought for the lost; but with force and with severity you have dominated them (Ezekiel 34:3-4).

God continues on to say that as a result the sheep are scattered and are thus easy prey to the beasts of the field.

In the church today the shepherd of the flock is called pastor, which literally means shepherd. Among the 12 disciples, Peter was probably the one that had the most sensitivity to this issue. During Jesus' interrogation by the Pharisees, Peter denied Him three times. Among Jesus' appearances to the 11 after His resurrection was one where Jesus instructed Peter to "feed My sheep" and "tend to My lambs."[1] It is Peter, then, who writes to the church, "Therefore, I exhort the elders[2] among you... shepherd the flock of God among you, exercising oversight, not under compulsion, but voluntarily, according to the will of God; and not for sordid gain, but with eagerness" (I Peter 5:1-2).

It is hard for those who have never suffered abuse like Michael Reagan and millions of others to comprehend the long term impact of childhood abuse. What is even worse, like the man on the telephone, there are thousands of men and women who refuse to have anything to do with the church and Christianity because they were abused, sexually and otherwise, by pastors and elders in the church. I believe that what the Roman Catholic Church is going through right now with the revelation of sexual abuse by priests (and nuns) is only the tip of the iceberg. And it is not limited to the Roman Catholic Church by any means. The other cases have simply not gotten the same level of national publicity.

Even worse is the abuse by parents, relatives, teachers, and other adults in responsible positions. It is hard to calculate the immense damage done in the lives of their victims. They are predators, with children as their prey. Many of them are professing Christians.

There are other ways, too, in which church leadership abuse the flock. Some impose burdens of guilt in order to extract money. They place men and women under yokes of bondage that they themselves cannot bear so that they continue in their positions of dominance.

Some use their position of responsibility to lord it over others, making themselves appear important. The Pharisees of Jesus' day were good at that, but so are many in our churches today.

Jesus cries, "Woe to you!"

> *Whoever causes one of these little ones* [a child, a new believer] *who believe in Me to stumble, it is better for him that a heavy millstone be hung around his neck, and that he be drowned in the depth of the sea* (Matthew 18:6).

He ends this parable by saying that when He returns and finds these wicked ones, the master "will cut him to pieces and assign him a place with the hypocrites." What a terrible judgment!

Jesus is standing at the door, but perhaps there is still time. It is easier to be an executive officer of an organization than to be a shepherd. God never called pastors to be the CEOs of large churches. He called them to shepherd His people and feed them.

On a broader scale, all of us who are placed in positions of leadership in the household of God are called to be servants in that household. Jesus gave us the example, when on the very night that He was betrayed, assumed the position of the lowest household slave and washed the feet of His disciples.

God has equipped each one with the ability to minister His grace as servants. Peter writes, "As each one has received a special gift, employ it in serving one another, as good stewards of the manifold grace of God" (I Peter 4:10). It is important that we discover how to serve and build each other up, so that when Jesus comes He will find us doing what we are supposed to be doing. That way we will never need to fear when He comes.

CHAPTER NOTES

[1] See John 21:15-17.

[2] The word here is the same root for the presbytery, or those who lead the church.

CHAPTER 8

No Excuses

*Be on the alert then, for you do not know
the day or the hour* (Matthew 25:13).

I grew up in a good home with an older brother and younger sister. Every day we all had certain chores to do, such as make our beds. There were some days, usually on Saturday, when we were given a special list of chores to do while my parents went grocery shopping. It was expected that those chores would be done by the time they got home.

As a child I much preferred playing to working, and on more than one occasion, I decided to play before doing the chores. The problem with that was that sometimes I got so caught up in the playing that I forgot the working, until I heard the car door close outside. At that point, however, it was too late. No matter how fast I moved, I could not get those chores done before my mother walked through the door.

Then the kingdom of heaven will be comparable to ten virgins, who took their lamps, and went out to meet the bridegroom. And five of them were foolish, and five were prudent. For when the foolish took their lamps, they took no oil with them, but the prudent took oil in flasks along with their lamps. ... But at midnight there was a shout, "Behold, the bridegroom! Come out to meet him." Then all those vir-

gins arose and trimmed their lamps. And the foolish said to the prudent, "Give us some of your oil, for our lamps are going out." But the prudent answered, saying, "No, there will not be enough for us and you too; go instead to the dealers, and buy some for your-selves."...the bridegroom came, and those who were ready went in with him to the wedding feast; and the door was shut (Matthew 25:1-13).

The Wedding

As was often the case when Jesus told parables, He used common occurrences that were familiar to His listeners. In this parable Jesus used the traditional Jewish wedding as the backdrop.

A typical marriage in Israel took place in three stages, sometimes spread out over a long period of time. The first step was the engagement, which was actually a negotiation between a representative of the potential bridegroom and the father of the bride. When the negotiations were concluded successfully, the betrothal, which was the second step, took place. These steps quite often were taken quite early in the life of the bride, while she was still a child.

When the betrothal was concluded, it was considered to be a legally binding agreement, and the couple was considered to be man and wife. Thus in Matthew 1:19 Joseph is considered to be the "husband" of Mary, although the marriage ceremony had not yet taken place. The only way a betrothal could be ended was through the process of issuing a bill of divorcement.

Since the bride was usually quite young at the time of the betrothal, the time between the betrothal and the marriage ceremony was quite long, often many years. The bride continued to live in the home of her parents, and the bridegroom went to prepare a place in which they would live once they were married. When he was ready and could support his wife, the bridegroom would assemble an entourage of friends, and they would go and fetch his bride.

In the meantime, the bride did not know exactly when the bridegroom was going to appear, and once she become of age, she had to be ready at all times. It was common to have some friends with her to help her watch.

When the time had come, the bridegroom would set out for the village of the bride and send a crier ahead of him to announce his coming. Since the wedding was most often performed at night, it was important to be prepared with plenty of light in the form of torches or oil lamps. In fact, anyone who did not have a lighted torch was not allowed in the procession.

The crier gave the bride sufficient time to awaken, if she was asleep, and prepare herself. When the bridegroom reached the house, the entire party of the bride and her attendants would go out to meet him and march joyously through the streets of the town to the location of the marriage and the marriage feast. Only those who were in the procession at the time it arrived at the wedding were allowed to enter. Once the doors were closed anyone else was considered a stranger and was not allowed in.

Too Late

The focus of this parable is not so much on the bride, the bridegroom, or even the wedding itself, but rather on the friends of the bride, i.e. the virgins. It was the duty and responsibility of the friends to be prepared for the arrival of the bridegroom. That they were sleeping was also not unusual or an issue.

Central to the point that Jesus was making is the

conversation that took place between the two groups of friends. One group of five made sure they were prepared with extra oil; the other group did not make any special preparations.

In this context, oil symbolizes spiritual preparation. When the time came and the second group recognized they did not have enough oil, they asked the others for some of theirs. The other group refused, however, not because they did not want to help, but because they couldn't transfer oil from one person to the other and be ready themselves. At a spiritual level, transferring oil would be impossible.

Note that both groups—those that had enough oil and those who did not—had the same amount of time to prepare, and both had the same amount of knowledge of what was about to happen. The problem with those who were not prepared was not with the bride, the bride-groom, the time of the wedding, or the other virgins. It was rather that they chose not to be prepared, even though they knew it was expected of them.

It is like when I as a child given a list of chores to do. I eventually learned that the best thing to do is to finish the chores first, then play. Then, when I heard the car door close, I did not have to worry.

Once the bridegroom appeared and everyone else joined the procession it was too late for the foolish virgins to prepare. When they finally arrived at the place of the wedding after eventually finding someone who could sell them some oil, the doors were closed. It was as if they were total strangers.

In the Body of Christ we all have the same opportunity and time. No one has an advantage over another. There are certain things we need to be doing now that cannot be delayed until the time the Bridegroom comes.

One of these things is in the area of lifestyle. We as believers must adopt a lifestyle of developing within us the characteristics of Jesus. As Peter writes,

> *Now for this very reason also, applying all diligence, in your faith supply moral excellence, and in your moral excellence, knowledge; and in your knowledge, self-control, and in your self-control, perseverance, and in your perseverance, godliness; and in your godliness, brotherly kindness, and in your brotherly kindness,* [Christian] *love* (II Peter 1:5-7).

The word used in the verse above is *agape*. Christian love is not a noun or a verb, but an adverb. It is not something I do or possess, but it is something I become. In I Corinthians 13, the famous "love chapter," Paul says that it does not matter much what we do or say if it is done without Christian love.

Like the foolish virgins, if we discover we do not have these things we need, they cannot be transferred from another, nor can they be developed quickly.

The other thing we need to be aware of is in the area of service, or ministry, in the body. As Paul says in I Corinthians 12, each member of the body has a unique and important function to perform. The function of the attendants was to serve the bride so that she would be ready when the bridegroom came for her.

We must be sure of our calling—our function and area of service—in the body of Christ. It is not so much that we do what we decide we want to do, but rather we get serious with God and find out what He has for us to do. As we saw in the last parable, we are the bond-slaves in the household, and He is the Lord and Master.

In the continuation of the passage from II Peter quoted above, Peter goes on to say,

Therefore, brethren, be all the more diligent to make certain about His calling and choosing you; for as long as you practice these things, you will never stumble; for in this way the entrance into the eternal kingdom [also read as door to the wedding feast] of our Lord and Savior Jesus Christ will be abundantly supplied to you (II Peter 1:10-11).

One of the reasons many Christians struggle so much in their relationship with Jesus is that they are not functioning properly in the body of Christ. Many of us feel useless and see ourselves serving no useful purpose beyond, perhaps, putting an offering in the basket. When that happens, we get careless in our walk with Jesus.

Peter says that when we do the things that Jesus has equipped us to do we will not stumble. When we were born again into the Kingdom of God, we were created for good works which God created for us (Ephesians 2:10). These go far beyond obeying the Ten Commandments. They are spiritual good works which God has ordained for us and uniquely equipped us to perform. For myself, when I am about my Father's business doing what He has called me to do, I pray more, am more attentive to His voice, and struggle with sin less.

Both lifestyle and ministry require diligence on our part; they do not simply happen automatically. We must be about our Father's business, so that when Jesus, the bridegroom, returns we will have plenty of oil for our lamps. Do not wait until the last minute to get started, for then it will be too late.

CHAPTER 9

Graceful Talents

For through the grace given to me I say... (Romans
12:3).

The prophet Elijah was going through a difficult
time. God had called him to declare a drought
on the land, and now he found himself without
food or water. Again God spoke and told him to leave
Israel. He was to go to a foreign place near the city of
Sidon, and there he would meet a widow who would provide food and water for him.

When he arrived at the widow's home, it was quickly
apparent in their conversation, that although she was
willing to do what she could for the man of God, she had
almost nothing to give him. In fact, she and her young
son were at the point of starvation and had but a small
bit of flour and oil, the staples of their diet. Nevertheless,
what she had, she was willing to give.

What happened next was a miracle. No matter how
much flour she took out of the bowl, it never was empty,
and no matter how much oil she poured out of the jar,
there was always more. Not only did she have enough to
feed the prophet of God, but she had more than enough
to feed herself and son. (This story is found in I Kings
17:1-16)

For it is just like a man about to go on a journey, who called his own slaves, and entrusted his possessions to them. And to one he gave five talents, to another two, and to another, one, each according to his ability; and he went on his journey. ...Now after a long time the master of those slaves came and settled accounts with them. And the one who had received the five talents came up and brought five more talents ...The one also who had received the two talents ...said, "I have gained two more talents." And the one also who had received the one talent came up and said, "I was afraid, and went away and hid your talent in the ground" (Matthew 25:14-30).

Talents

You may have noticed that there has been something of a progression in these parables. It started with the need to respond in faith to the prophetic word; from there Jesus talked of the necessity of being spiritually alert and awake. In the last two parables, Jesus spoke of something more that is required of us. Now in this parable of the talents, He continues to develop this idea.

Perhaps we have difficulty with the idea that Jesus expects something of us. So much of our Christian doctrine centers around what Jesus has and continues to do for us that we find if strange to our ears that He would place high expectations on us doing something. If we were to stand back and look at our attitudes, it would seem that the roles of master and slave are sometimes reversed. We often demand of God that He fulfill His promises of blessing on us as if we are the ones in control.

The bond between Jesus and the believer is one of love—His love for us and our love for Him. It is out of the motivation of that love that we enter into the relationship of Lord and liege, Master and servant. His love never changes towards us, and it is out of love that He provides all good things. He also has the right to expect obedience on our part.

The story of this parable is straightforward. A master is about to leave on a long journey, so he calls the slaves of his household and distributes some of his money to each one. They are free to use it while he is gone, but when he returns he will expect an accounting. There are some features of this parable, however, that require some comment.

- The master represents Jesus, and the bond-slaves are the saints. There does not seem to be any hint here that his distribution is only to certain ones. All of them were included.
- The master divides his wealth among them, but he does not give each one an equal portion. A talent has nothing to do with an innate ability, such as playing the piano or singing. It was a unit of measure, probably on the order of 100 pounds of silver, which represents about 15 years worth of wages for a laborer. In today's economy in the United States this would be in excess of $250,000, a large amount of money. That meant that even the one who received only one talent still had a very large sum of money.
- The master divided his wealth among them "each according to his own ability." It was not discriminatory in a negative sense that they did not all receive the same amount. Rather it was a blessing, for to give one more than he could handle would put him in a position of failure.
- The bond-slaves were stewards of this wealth, they did not own it. The money was a resource and was entrusted to them for a purpose, which each one knew.
- The bond-slaves did not earn this wealth; it was given to them as a free gift, which they could use in any way they wanted.

- The master expected a return on his investment. Even the one who was given only one talent had an enormous resource which was capable of a significant return.

Grace

Although it is quite common for commentators to use this parable as a lesson in handling finances, I believe Jesus' intent had nothing to do with money. Money only represents the resource to do something. The currency of the kingdom of heaven is not money or wealth; it is grace.

We normally think of grace as the unmerited favor of God, and it is that. As Paul says in his letter to the Ephesians, "By grace you have been saved." We do not earn salvation; it is a free gift from God. By God's grace, His kindness towards us, He moved us from being a slave of sin to a place of righteousness in Christ Jesus, from Satan's kingdom of darkness to God's kingdom of light.

Grace is much more than that, however. It is the ability and the resources to do what God has called us to do. God never expects us to live according to our natural resources and abilities. He calls those things works of the flesh. Instead He equips us with His grace. Consider these statements by Paul:

And since we have gifts that differ according to the grace given to us, let each exercise them accordingly (Romans 12:6).

According to the grace of God, which was given to me, like a wise master builder I laid a foundation, and another is building on it (I Corinthians 3:10).

[The gospel to the Gentiles] *of which I was made a*

61

minister, according to the gift of God's grace which was given to me according to the working of His power. To me, the very least of all saints, this grace was given to me to preach to the Gentiles the unfathomable riches of Christ (Ephesians 3:8).

But to each one of us grace was given according to the measure of Christ's gift (Ephesians 4:7).

That was the lesson of the encounter between Elijah and the widow. God's provision, His grace, was not a question of what resources were available in the natural. When the widow believed the word of the Lord and used the resources she already had, she discovered that God's grace had no limit.

Notice the relationship between the master giving the talents to the bond-slaves and God giving grace to Paul for ministry. In spite of all his education and training, Paul admitted to himself and others that he was weak, and it was only God's equipping grace that enabled him to be effective. We can substitute "grace" for "talents" in the parable and get a sense of what grace is all about.

- The Master divides His grace among us. Even the smallest amount of grace is an enormous resource.
- Not all are given an equal amount of grace, but the Master distributes to each according to His purpose and our ability.
- Jesus gives to each one grace according to his ability. It is a mistake to look at the grace working in the life of another and conclude that you must be the same as him. We must find that unique way in which God has given us grace to minister in the body of Christ.
- Grace does not belong to us. We are stewards of grace,

and it is given to us as a resource, not a possession.

• We do not earn grace, but grace can be multiplied in our life as we exercise what has been given to us.

• God expects to see some results of His grace, and He will call us to account. The more one has been given, the more that is expected of him.

Results

When the master returned, he gathered the slaves together and inquired of each one what the results were. The first two came and returned to the master double of what they were given. They took risks in using this wealth. It is a principle of investing that the greater the return, the greater the risks. Some of their attempts probably resulted in failure, but some returned incredible dividends. In the end they discovered that over a period of time they had increased their investment considerably.

The third one had a different attitude. He was like the foolish virgins in that he did not do what was necessary or expected. He wanted to see concrete evidence of the outcome before he would invest any of the money. Since that was not possible, he hid his resources and refused to use them at all, even in low risk ventures. Furthermore, as he saw no fruit, no increase in the amount of his gift, he blamed the master for giving it to him.

Since the talents represent grace, then the attitude that the first two slaves had of being willing to take risks represents faith. Exercising faith involves risk. It means stepping outside of our comfort zone and putting ourselves in situations that go beyond our natural abilities. Sometimes we will not succeed in our own eyes, but that is not the end of grace. More importantly, sometimes we do succeed, and we begin to better understand where and how the grace is working in our lives.

One of the exciting results of taking spiritual risks is to see how God works. Some think they cannot do anything unless Jesus comes and gives them specific instructions on who, what, when, and how to do it. Yet in this parable the master did not tell the slaves what to do with the money; they just knew what was expected. If we are so afraid of doing the wrong thing that we do nothing, consider the fact that you cannot steer an automobile that is standing still. Likewise, as long as we are standing still doing nothing, God cannot change our direction.

We are all equal in value in the sight of Jesus, since God is no respecter of persons. However, we are not all equal in function and gifting. Once we find where grace has been given to us, then we need to operate in that grace whenever and wherever we can.

Discovering our grace giftings can happen through revelation and experience. It helps to find a mentor, a spiritual father/mother, who can help us discover and use our grace gifts. It will also happen through trial and error, as we look and see where we did and did not function in the grace of Jesus. As with the good slaves in this parable, when we depend upon God's grace, we will see the grace in our lives begin to grow.

Sometimes I have wondered what the reaction of the master would have been if the third slave had come to him and said that he tried to invest the money, but ended up losing everything. I think it would have been far more tolerable than it was for him not trying at all. The good news is that, while it is possible to lose a financial investment, it is impossible for grace not to bear dividends.

Why do we look at our own perceived strengths and

abilities as if this is what we have to rely upon? Paul chastised the Galatians for this way of thinking.

You foolish Galatians, who has bewitched you?...Are you so foolish? Having begun by the Spirit [grace], *are you now being perfected by the flesh?* (Galatians 3:1,3)

God's grace is immensely greater than we have experienced or can even imagine.

CHAPTER 10

Rewarding Influence

You are the salt of the earth...the light of the world...
(Matthew 5:13,14).

The story of Corrie ten Boom is well known. In her famous book, *The Hiding Place,* she described how her family risked everything to aid and assist Jews being persecuted by the Nazi Germans during World War II. Because of their strong Christian faith, love, and devotion, Corrie's family was responsible for saving scores of Jewish people. Today, Corrie is honored as a "Righteous Gentile" in the *Yad Vashem,* the Holocaust Museum, in Israel. The walkway leading up to the museum is lined with carob trees, each of which is dedicated to the memory of a "Righteous Gentile." Among them is one dedicated to Corrie ten Boom.

Not all those honored in this way were Christians. Each one had their own reasons, but all are honored the same way and are held in high esteem in Israel.

Judgment

But when the Son of Man comes in His glory...then He will sit on His glorious throne. And all the nations will be gathered before Him; and He will separate them one from another, as the shepherd separates the sheep from the goats (Matthew 25:31-32).

The parable of the sheep and the goats, which is the final parable that Jesus told in the Olivet Discourse has to do with the judgment of the nations. This is not so much a parable as it is a straightforward description of what Jesus will do when He establishes His millennial kingdom.

By way of review, during the tribulation Satan will be permitted to have his way and persecute both Christians and Jews. In so doing he will be actually purifying the people of God. When Jesus perceives that Satan has done enough, He will remove the remaining saints and sequester the faithful remnant of the Jews in a safe place in the wilderness.[1] At this point, Jesus will begin to bring the wrath of God onto those who have sided with Satan.

Satan's reaction to God's wrath will be to assemble the nations of the world in Israel and attempt to wage war on Jesus. In spite of this great military might, the armies at Armageddon will be no match for Jesus. Jesus will come with the armies of heaven, clothed in white linen,[2] and He will destroy the nations assembled with the sharp sword of His mouth (Revelation 19:14-15). The Antichrist and his false prophet will be thrown into the lake of fire for everlasting torment, and all those "who had received the mark of the beast and those who worshiped his image…[will be] killed with the sword which came from the mouth of Him [Jesus]" (Revelation 19:20-21).

At this point, Jesus will establish His kingdom, His government, on the earth, with His throne in Jerusalem. There will be three groups of people on the earth at this time: the saints, who have come with Jesus in the armies of heaven; the faithful remnant of Israel; and the many people remaining on the earth who did not take the mark of the beast and worship his image. It is this last group which is the subject of this parable.

When Jesus is sitting on His throne in Jerusalem, He will gather the nations before Him. The word translated "nations" here is *ethnos* in the Greek, from which we derive the English word ethnic. It is most often translated "Gentiles" and does not include either the saints or the descendents of Israel.

There are, perhaps, many reasons why these people will not take the mark of the beast and worship his image, but it is important that they will not. If they did, they would not be able to stand before Jesus. They would be included with those who will be slain by the sword of Jesus' mouth. However, they will have to face one more test.

Jesus will divide these people into two groups based upon how they will have treated the saints and/or the Jews during the time of the tribulation as the Antichrist seeks them out to kill them. Those who will have compassion on the ones being persecuted and will meet their needs will be welcomed into the kingdom. Those who will not will be consigned to everlasting punishment.

Reward

Jesus told us that we are to be the salt of the earth and the light of the world. Being salt and light is not so much in what we say as in what we do. The adage that actions speak louder than words certainly applies as others see how we live. During the tribulation, being salt and light is going to take on a new dimension. How will we handle adversity? How will we conduct ourselves?

There are going to be many who, although they are not Christians themselves, observe our behavior as we are being persecuted and will be deeply touched. Consider how Peter challenged the believers:

> *Beloved, I urge you as aliens and strangers to abstain from fleshly lusts, which wage war against the soul. Keep your behavior excellent among the Gentiles, so that in the thing in which they slander you as evildoers, they may on account of your good deeds, as they observe them, glorify God in the day of visitation* [Christ's coming again in judgment] (I Peter 2:11-12).

One of the tactics that persecutors of the church have always used is to slander believers and twist our doctrines to make it appear that we are evil. The purpose for this is to turn public opinion against us and thus create a climate where persecutions are deemed to be beneficial to the people. This was often done, for example, during the Roman persecutions of the second and third centuries. Lies were spread about the Christians, even to the extent of saying that they would kill babies and drink their blood.

In spite of these attempts to cast Christianity in such an unfavorable light, it did not work. This is how Foxe described one such persecution.

> Nero, finding that a severe odium was cast upon him [for the burning of Rome], determined to charge the whole upon the Christians, at once to excuse himself and have an opportunity of fresh persecutions. But the savagery of this inhuman monster, so far from crushing out the faith, which he hated, only tended, in God's good providence, to its extension. The charred ruins of the noble Circus, the bleeding bodies of the slaughtered Christians, the desolated city, when contrasted with the meek, inoffensive lives of those

who suffered such tortures, and to whose account the tyrant dared to lay the destruction of that city, exercised an influence amongst the people in favour of Christianity.[3]

It is possible that many who observe the persecution of God's people during the tribulation will be deeply touched, and although they never commit themselves to Jesus as Lord, they aid and give comfort to those being persecuted. Perhaps it will be like the people, living in the Nazi occupied countries during World War II, who risked everything to protect and save the Jews.

Jesus is quite clear that those who do help believers will receive the reward of living in His earthly kingdom. Those who refuse to do so will be consigned to eternal punishment. Yet some of the responsibility for that rests on our shoulders. What will they see when they look at us?

This is true even today. People around us who would never go to a church meeting are looking at us to see how we live and behave. They notice immediately when our words are in conflict with our actions. People do not want to hear what we have to say until they know how much we love them. Our influence is not in the halls of government or in the courts of law—it is in the hearts of people.

Let your light shine before men in such a way that they may see your good works, and glorify your Father who is in heaven (Matthew 5:16).

CHAPTER NOTES

[1] This is the woman fleeing into the wilderness in Revelation 12:6, 13-16.

[2] These are the tribulation saints, those who were martyred and those who were raptured together.

[3] *Foxe's Book of Martyrs*, Marie Gentert King, ed., Spire Books (1975), p. 14.

CHAPTER 11

The Challenge

We are not going to...worship the golden
image (Daniel 3:18).

I t had been a difficult time for the four men. When they were not yet teenagers the invading armies of Nebuchadnezzar conquered their land and subjected their people to a harsh rule. They themselves were torn from their families and everything that was familiar to them, and taken hundreds of miles to a strange city in a strange land to live in the court of their conqueror.

In the midst of this tragedy, they had three choices: 1) They could become bitter and lament the injustice of what had happened. They were, after all, just victims of something for which they bore no responsibility. 2) They could try to make the best of the situation and be assimilated into the culture and life of the court. Life in the court had its advantages, but they would have to give up their own identity and heritage as God's people. 3) They could be redemptive, seeking God's hand and how He was going to use them in this situation. Of the three choices, this one was the most difficult and the one most fraught with danger, since it might require them to go against the prevailing culture.

From the beginning, however, they had determined to

be faithful to God and to try and follow His directions. And from the beginning, their resolve was put to the test. It was not easy living in the midst of wealth and luxury, surrounded by people who worshipped other gods.

Soon after their arrival, they were given food that was not lawful for them to eat. What would they do? Based upon the decision they had already made, they refused the food, and God granted them favor in the sight of their overseers.

Years later, the circumstances had changed; they were no longer boys and strangers in a strange land, but had become well known and highly respected men. God had given them superior wisdom and insight, and they all held high government positions with the commensurate benefits and privileges. And yet three of them were now facing a difficult, even life threatening, situation.

King Nebuchadnezzar had declared himself to be a god. He had built a huge golden statue of himself and set it in a large open area. Assembling the leaders together, he declared that at the given signal, everyone must bow down and worship the statue of himself. The penalty for not worshipping the statue was death.

Everything was on the line for the three Jewish men. To worship the image was to deny and dishonor the name of the God of Abraham, Isaac, and Jacob; to refuse to worship the image meant certain death.

Their minds had been made up, however, long before the statue was erected. Their decision had actually been made many years before, and now it was just a matter of acting on that decision. When the king offered an opportunity for them to change their minds, their response was to say that it would do no good, that their minds were made up. They went on to say,

If we are thrown into the blazing furnace, the God whom we serve is able to save us. He will rescue us from your power, Your Majesty. But even if he doesn't, Your Majesty can be sure that we will never serve your gods or worship the gold statue you have set up (Daniel 3:17-18, *New Living Bible*).

This, of course, is the well known story of Shadrach, Meshach, and Abednego found in Daniel chapters 1-3. This story of the three faithful men in the fiery furnace illustrates the subject of this book. There are strong similarities between what happened in Nebuchadnezzar's day and what is going to happen in the day of the Antichrist.

Decisions, particularly those made in a crisis, are never made in a vacuum. They are the result of much training and the many decisions that were made over the months and years preceding the crisis. The times when we find ourselves in the middle of crisis situations are not the times to think about how to respond. That decision must be made well in advance.

We live in dangerous times today. There is a widespread consensus among evangelicals today that we are rapidly approaching the time of Jesus' return, that time the Bible refers to as "the day of the Lord." While that is an exciting prospect, it also means that as Christians we face a treacherous enemy. Satan speaks with many voices and seeks to deceive and mislead as many as he can, especially believers. The body of Jesus Christ is going to be sorely tested, and many are going to fail the test. For those who, in spite of everything, pass the test and remain faithful to their calling, the rewards are stupendous.

Are we up to the challenge that will soon face us as

Christians and the church? It is a question that we need to answer now. When difficult times come, it may be too late.

God has given us some clear directions as to what we can do as individuals and churches in order that we will be prepared ahead of time. Like Shadrach, Meshach, Abednego, and Daniel, who made the life and death decisions years before they were required to act upon them, we also need to prepare ourselves now for an uncertain future.

Providentially, we do not have to do this on our own. We have others to whom the Lord of the Harvest has joined us. The church, the body of Christ, is God's provision for us.

The next section looks at the first three chapters of Revelation, which is the instruction of Jesus to the church for the times to come.

CHAPTER 12

The Great Preparation

*Write in a book what you see, and send it
to the...churches* (Revelation 1:11).

I n the early 1950s, after it was discovered that the
Soviet Union also possessed nuclear weapons and
had the ability to deliver them, thousands of people
built bomb shelters and stocked them with food and
water in order to survive a nuclear attack, if it should
occur. That was their response as individuals to the
threat.

The government also had plans. Each locality had
what was known as a Civil Defense Program, which was
an organized approach to help citizens survive any attack of the perceived enemy. Special routes were
mapped out and designated by color—the blue or red
route—to aid in evacuation procedures. As school children, we regularly went through drills that taught us
where to go and what to do in the event of a nuclear attack.

Looking back on these things now, knowing what we
do about the power of nuclear bombs, it is easy to see
how inadequate our preparations were. They were
simply an attempt by a responsible government to provide for its citizens.

Jesus is the Head of His body, the Church. As such,

He would not be so inconsiderate as to leave the Church without plans of preparation for the difficult times in the tribulation. Just as the parables He told in the Olivet Discourse can be considered prophetically as instruction to us as individual believers, the first three chapters of Revelation provide His warnings and instruction to the church on how to prepare for the time to come.

The prophetic nature of these letters is further emphasized by the way Jesus looked and where He was standing when He appeared to John.

His Likeness

When Jesus was in heaven with His Father and the Holy Spirit at the time of creation, He was God, not man. The Bible testifies that God is spirit, and while He sometimes manifested Himself in the physical creation, His essence is spiritual not physical. Paul, however, reminded the church that Jesus set His godhead aside; He "emptied himself" and took on the form of a man (Philippians 2:6-7). It is not that Jesus' manhood was an illusion whereby He pretended to be a man while somehow preserving the option that at anytime He could change back. Rather, He gave up His godhead altogether and took on all the limitations of man, except one.

Jesus was born without sin, and because He walked in perfect obedience to His heavenly Father all His life, sin was never found in Him (see II Corinthians 5:21; Hebrews 5:15). Jesus was crucified and died upon the cross, further demonstrating that He had to be a man, since God could not die.

When He was resurrected from the dead, He was resurrected with a body. He forever changed, not the nature of God, but the nature of mankind. John said it this way: "As many as received Him, to them He gave the right to become *children of God*, even to those who believe in His name" (John 1:12, emphasis added). Jesus became like us so that through Him we might become like Him. When we are "born again" through Jesus, we take on His nature. This is what Paul was referring to when he wrote, "if any man is in Christ, he is a new creature; the old things have passed away; behold, new things have come" (II Corinthians 5:17). When Jesus walked this earth, He performed signs, wonders, and miracles. He did these, not as God, but as a man filled with the power of the Holy Spirit (Luke 4:14). This is the hope that we have, that as we are in Jesus, we also can walk like Him in the power of the Holy Spirit.

After His resurrection the disciples and others touched him; Thomas put his fingers into the nail holes in His hands and the hole in His side caused by the centurion's spear. It was in this same form of a man when He was taken up into heaven. The testimony of the angels is that Jesus "will come in just the same way [manner] as you have watched Him go into heaven" (Acts 1:11). He did not revert back to the form He had at creation and before His incarnation. He retained His physical form, and that is what John saw.

When John first saw Jesus that day on the island of Patmos in the Aegean Sea off the coast of what is now Turkey, He was "like a son of man" (Revelation 1:13). Jesus looked powerful, with a "voice like the sound of a trumpet" (v. 10); His eyes were "like a flaming fire" (v. 14); "His feet like burnished bronze" (v. 15); and "out of His mouth came a sharp two-edged sword" (v. 16).

Jesus' incarnation was not temporary. When He returns with the saints and the angels to lead the sons of Israel into victory over the Antichrist at Armageddon,

He will do so in the same body He had when we ascended. When He rules in the Millennial Kingdom, He will literally sit on the throne of David.

Moreover, those who are alive in Jesus and remain faithful can look forward to having the same form as Jesus: "Just as we have borne the image of the earthy, we shall also bear the image of the heavenly" (I Corinthians 15:49).

Among the Lampstands

In John's vision, Jesus is standing among seven lampstands, which are later identified as being the seven churches (v. 20). The word found here, translated in the New Testament from the Greek as "lampstands," would be rendered *menorah* in the Old Testament Hebrew. The menorah was the lampstand found in the Tabernacle. The lampstands have symbolic meanings, and in the symbolism of the menorah there is contained some of the characteristics of the church.

There were two primary areas that made up the Tabernacle: the Outer Court and the Sanctuary. The Outer Court was the location of the Altar of Sacrifice, representing Jesus' crucifixion, and the Laver, which represents the fact that Jesus, the Living Word of God, washes us clean from sin.

Located inside the Outer Court was the Sanctuary, a building about 15 feet wide, 45 feet long, and 15 feet high. The Sanctuary was divided into two rooms: the Holy Place and the Holy of Holies. The Holy of Holies occupied the back third of the Sanctuary and contained the Ark of the Covenant, on top of which was the Mercy Seat. It was entered only one time during the year so that the priest could minister the blood of the lamb on the Mercy Seat for the forgiveness of sins.

The Holy Place contained three pieces of furniture. One of the ways to understand the significance of the Holy Place is to see it was a model of the church. The Table of Showbread was located on the north wall and contained 12 loaves of bread, one for each of the 12 tribes of Israel. Remember that Jesus said, "I am the bread of life" (John 6:35). Just as the bread broken in the Lord's Supper represents His body broken for us, the church is also the body of Jesus, broken for the world. The second piece of furniture was the Altar of Incense, which speaks of worship and intercession. Finally the third piece of furniture was the Golden Lampstand or Menorah.

The Menorah was the only source of light in the Holy Place. This light came from the burning of a specially prepared oil, representative of the Holy Spirit. In the Sermon on the Mount, Jesus instructed His listeners that they are the light of the world and that this light must not be hidden. It is the purpose of light to reveal things hidden by the darkness. Likewise, it is the purpose of the church, as the Body of Christ, to reveal the person and work of Jesus to a world lost in darkness. When the world looks at the church, they are to see Jesus.

There is more symbolism to the light from the Menorah than that, however. The source of the light is the oil, i.e. the Holy Spirit, demonstrating that the source of revelation is God, not our human understanding and intellect. Our western civilization, with its emphasis on human intellect and reasoning, largely rejects supernatural revelation. Yet the light that comes from the Holy Spirit is that of revelation in the spirit, not comprehension with the mind. During the tribulation of the last days, supernatural revelation is going to play an important role in survival. Those who do not know how to "hear the Lord" are going to be in danger.

Furthermore, the oil in the Menorah had to be replenished daily. Yesterday's revelation is good, but it may not be enough to carry us through tomorrow. Jesus instructed His disciples, and thus us, with the admonition to be filled with the Holy Spirit.

Finally, consider how the Menorah was made. The other two pieces of furniture, the Table of Showbread and the Altar of Incense, were made of acacia wood covered in gold. Acacia wood is representative of humanity and its fallen nature, while gold is representative of divinity. The acacia wood was nowhere exposed to view but was covered completely in gold, which signifies the divine nature of Jesus and His shed blood covering our sinful nature. However, the Menorah was not made of wood, but was pure gold.

The church is a mystery. Although the church has structure, it is not a human institution that was somehow transformed by God. It is not a group of people coming together one or two days a week in a building to sing songs and hear a sermon. It is not a governmental assembly trying to hammer out doctrine so that one group is distinct from another. Like the menorah, the church is pure gold; it is not human, but supernatural. The light and revelation that the church puts forth in the world are not to be a mixture of the human and divine, but rather they are to be pure.

The Bible uses several different illustrations to try and explain this mystery. The apostle Paul called the church a building "growing into a holy temple in the Lord; in whom you also are being built together into a dwelling of God in the Spirit" (Ephesians 2:21-22). Peter declared that we "as living stones, are being built up as a spiritual house for a holy priesthood, to offer up spiritual sacrifices acceptable to God through Jesus Christ" (I Peter 2:5).

In other places the Bible uses an illustration of a body, with Jesus the head, where all the parts of the body are joined together and dependent upon one another for life. This body is an organic whole, not a collection of parts like some Frankenstein. For example, Paul writes, "There should be no division in the body, but that the members should have the same care for one another" (I Corinthians 12:25). Paul is not speaking about some local assembly; there is only one Body.

The tribulation will be a dangerous time for believers, and they are often going to be called upon to be willing to give their lives. Believers are going to be pressed on all sides, and it is not going to be enough for them to be loyal to the particular organization to which they belong. The church must be more like a family. People will not give their lives for the president or CEO of a corporation, but they will give their lives for sons and daughters, brothers and sisters.

Compare the life of the church in places where the church is being persecuted and where it is not. Where there is little or no persecution, the church is largely an institution. The perspective from an institution is that an organization is required to do just about any function of the church. Missionary activity requires mission societies; evangelism requires elaborate evangelistic outreaches and associations; teaching requires seminaries and Bible schools. Most church-goers today are identified more by their denomination, i.e. institution, than by any other characteristic. And most church-goers are relatively unfruitful, leaving it to the paid staff to do the ministry.

On the other hand, in places such as China, where the church has been heavily persecuted, the institutional church is almost absent. After the Communists had taken over China at the end of World War II, for example, there was tremendous persecution of believers. It was believed by many in the West that the church in China had ceased to exist. What has been discovered in recent years is that the church went underground, out of sight. Today it is estimated there are more than 100 million believers in China, and in the estimation of many, the Chinese church is the fastest growing one in the world.

This kind of growth is not a result of organization, but rather a result of function and relationship. It is the body of Christ living in small groups, supporting and discipling one another, being willing to sacrifice everything for their Savior and one another.

That Jesus was standing in the midst of the seven lampstands represents His concern about, His presence in, and His intimate knowledge of His church. It is in this context that He dictates letters to seven churches located in modern-day Turkey.

The Seven Letters

The book itself is addressed to "the seven churches that are in Asia" (v. 4). These were all actual churches where John had a personal relationship and had given apostolic oversight. As Jesus is seen standing among the lampstands, He has seven stars in His hand, which represent the seven "angels" in the seven churches. While angels are usually associated with the host in heaven that serves God, the word literally means "messenger."

It is unlikely that the sense here is of angels; more likely the sense is of messengers who, since John was restricted to the island, traveled from him to the churches to maintain communication.[3]

As Jesus dictates these letters, it is obvious that He also knows each one personally and is intimately aware of how they are. If this were the only importance of these churches, however, their inclusion here would be doubtful. It is more likely that these seven represent the church globally. The context of these letters is that they introduce the rest of the book of Revelation, which is the culmination of prophecy. So, while these are real letters to real churches, they are also seven letters to the church just prior to the commencement of the events that have just been outlined. In other words, these seven letters are prophetic.

Prophetically the letters represent seven types of churches in light of end times events. They range from the churches in Philadelphia and Smyrna, for whom Jesus has nothing negative to say, to the church at Sardis, for whom Jesus has the most severe warning. The prophetic purpose of these letters is two-fold: first as a warning, and then as an encouragement.

In the chapters that follow, each of the letters will be examined in the order Jesus dictated them.

CHAPTER NOTES

[1] Asia was the Roman province that we now know as western Turkey.

[2] For a more complete discussion, see *Created in the Image of God,* by this author.

[3] Unger, Merrill F., *New Unger's Bible Handbook,* Laridian (Cedar Rapids, Iowa), reference to Revelation 1:20.

CHAPTER 13

EPHESUS—Refocused Love

You have left your first love... (Revelation 2:4).

Ephesus was an important city in Asia. It had the best harbor in the province and was considered to be the gateway to Asia. It was also the center of worship for the Greek deity, Artemis, also known as Diana. The temple of Artemis there was considered to be one of the seven wonders of the ancient world.

Ephesus was also an important city to John. The church in the city was founded by Paul, who spent more time there than at any other church he birthed. Later, John moved to Ephesus, where he settled along with Mary, the mother of Jesus. After John was released from his exile on the island of Patmos, he returned to Ephesus, where he died a few years later.

Jesus opened His letter to the Ephesians by identifying Himself as the One who "walks among the seven golden lampstands." Jesus walks among the Church, and thus He knows each church part of the body intimately. It is He who is the Head, and He is aware of everything that has happened.

Something, however, had happened in the life of this church. Jesus spoke a word of correction to them:

But I have this against you, that you have left your

first love. Remember therefore from where you have
fallen, and repent and do the deeds you did at first
(Revelation 2:4-5).

As a fellowship "matures," the nature of the activities often changes. At first everyone is excited about Jesus and the new life He has given them. All that seems to matter is experiencing the presence of the Lord among them. The saints also enjoy being with one another, like being in a warm, loving family. They share life with Jesus and with each other.

There is a subtle thing that happens in the midst of that life. We begin by doing things for Jesus. Someone has an idea, and so there is a committee that is appointed. If there is a committee, then there needs to be a chairman, and soon a hierarchy is established. Over a period of time, the church is transformed from being a family to being an institution, where it is the work of the institution that is important. Hierarchy and structure are substituted for the life of the Spirit-led believer. Activities become the focus instead of a relationship with Jesus.

The following story illustrates the message that Jesus tried to communicate in His letter to the church in Ephesus.

Mary and Martha, along with their brother, Lazarus, were good friends of Jesus. They lived in the village of Bethany not far from Jerusalem, and Jesus often stayed at their house.

Jesus was traveling with His disciples and came through Bethany one day. When He stopped at Martha's house, she graciously invited Him in and began to prepare everything necessary to care for her guests. While Martha was busy, Jesus and the disciples went up on the roof where it was cooler and they could rest.

Before long, Mary joined Jesus on the roof, where He was sharing about the things of God. She just enjoyed being in His presence. This was the same Mary who anointed the feet of Jesus, and she was glad for this opportunity to hear Him teach.

Meanwhile, Martha was busy preparing the meal and was getting frustrated because Mary was not there to help her. There was so much to do and so little time, and it really began to get on her nerves. Finally, she was fed up and went to see Jesus. "Jesus," she began, "I have all this work to do, and Mary is not helping me at all. Tell her to come down here and help me out."

Jesus' response surprised her. "Martha, you are being distracted and worried, trying to do too many things. A lot of things are important, but there is only one thing that is necessary. Mary has chosen that one thing, which is enjoying My presence while I am with her, and I am not going to deny her this time."[1]

In many ways Jesus characterizes the church at Ephesus as being like Martha. It is not that doing things for Him is necessarily wrong. In fact, He commends them for their perseverance and correct doctrine. It does make a difference what we believe. Correct understanding of the scriptures is critical to the proper functioning of the church.

It is not that these things are bad, but when we get caught up in the doing of things, we turn our focus away from Jesus and onto ourselves. This is what happened to Martha. When we start focusing on all the work that needs to be done, we lose our focus on Jesus. We start functioning on the basis of our strength, not in the strength of the Holy Spirit. Then, like Martha, we get frustrated and weary.

There is a deception in all our activity. We make

things complicated and complex, and in so doing, find ourselves serving someone other than Jesus. Paul was concerned about this in the Corinthian church, when he wrote,

> *For I am jealous for you with a godly jealousy; for I betrothed you to one husband, that to Christ I might present you as a pure virgin. But I am afraid, lest as the serpent deceived Eve by his craftiness, your minds should be led astray from the simplicity and purity of devotion to Christ* (II Corinthians 11:2-3).

Institutionally we adopt a name that gives us more identification than belonging to Jesus. We also tend to adopt names and titles that seem to give us importance in the eyes of others.

I find this to be true when I am ministering in Africa. People ask me what organization I represent, but I do not go representing an organization. I go because that is what Jesus asked me to do. It is surprising how often people do not understand that idea.

In the book of Ephesians, especially the first chapter, Paul reminds us that it is really not about us; it is about Jesus. Paul repeatedly uses phrases such as "in Him," "through Jesus Christ," and "in Christ," which stand in sharp distinction to our own efforts. It is by His grace we are saved, not by our efforts, and even our ministry is a gift from Jesus. Paul makes it clear in chapter 4 that our ministry has little to do with any natural abilities we may have, but are grace-gifts. Even in spiritual warfare, it is the might of the Lord that does the work.

Walking in the flesh for the Ephesian church had to do with focusing on themselves and their deeds. Sometimes when we minister to and in the body of

Christ, we begin to look at these things as something we have done instead of something that Jesus does through us as servants. We shift our focus from Jesus to ourselves.

Jesus is calling the Church to repent of all their fleshly activity and return to "your first love." We need to accept the truth of what Jesus said to Martha, not as a rebuke, but as a refocusing. A good measure of what is important to us is to see where and how we spend our time and efforts. It has been said that we will always find time to do that which is important to us.

Jesus calls us to an intimacy with Him, to sit at His feet like Mary, and He does this both corporately and individually.

The reward for a renewed and intensified love for Jesus is a restoration of the kind of fellowship enjoyed by Adam and Eve in the Garden. Remember that when they sinned by disobeying God, their joyous, intimate fellowship with God was broken, and God was forced to eject them from the Garden so that they would not eat of the fruit of the Tree of Life.

Being born again of the Spirit and having the indwelling presence of Jesus allows us to once again experience that type of fellowship with God. That is what Jesus is calling the church in Ephesus, and us too, to share.

CHAPTER NOTES

[1] This incident is found in Luke 10:38-42.

CHAPTER 14

SMYRNA—Victorious Loss

"I will give you the crown of life." Revelation 2:10

O f all the cities in Asia[1], Smyrna was considered to be the most beautiful, but it was still a Roman colony. Persecution and violence toward the church there could flare up at any time, and often did. One of those occasions resulted in the martyrdom of Polycarp, famous Bishop of Smyrna, in 155 AD.[2]

Under torture a slave broke down and revealed the place where Polycarp was staying. When the soldiers came to arrest him, Polycarp ordered that they all be given a meal while he asked for the privilege of one hour in prayer. When they arrived at the city, he was taken to the arena where he was given the opportunity of declaring "Caesar is Lord," thereby denying Jesus. Polycarp's response was, "Eighty and six years have I served Him, and He has done me no wrong. How can I blaspheme my King who saved me?" The proconsul then threatened him with burning, and Polycarp replied, "You threaten me with fire that burns for a time and is quickly quenched, for you do not know the fire which awaits the wicked in the judgment to come and in everlasting punishment. Why are you waiting? Come, do what you will."

So the crowd began carrying pieces of wood from the city, and even though it was the Sabbath, the Jews were at the forefront. They were about to bind him to the stake, and he said, "Leave me as I am, for he who gives me power to endure the fire, will grant me to remain in the flames unmoved even without the security you will give by the nails." And that is the way he died.

Winning or Losing the War

When is a loss actually a victory? Is it ever true that you can lose the battle but in so doing win the war? Or conversely, you win the battle and thereby lose the war?

This is exactly the situation with the church in Smyrna. The letter that Jesus sent to Smyrna is the shortest of the seven, and Smyrna is one of two churches to whom He has nothing negative to say at all. They are in the midst of tribulation, and yet He promises them nothing but more tribulation at the hands of Satan. His purpose seems to be to encourage them to remain faithful.

One of the things that we have a difficult time understanding about the Kingdom of God is that it seems to operate backwards. Jesus said that if you want to live you must first die (Romans 8:13). Now He says that although they are poor, they are in fact rich.

In Smyrna the Christians were living in poverty. This was not being poor as we know it, but abject poverty. During times of persecution it was legal for people to simply take what they wanted from the Christians.

Perhaps this is one of the things that permits the persecuted church to flourish. Jesus said that you cannot serve both riches and God, because each one is a master. In an affluent society, we continue to think that we can do both in spite of what Jesus said. James warns that the love of money is the source of all kinds of evil, and during times of persecution it is exceedingly difficult to try to serve both masters.

How is it that Jesus can say they are rich in the midst of crushing poverty? It is because they are laying up for themselves treasures in heaven. Poverty in and of itself is not more spiritual than riches, but being in poverty because you are truly spiritual and are walking with Jesus is riches. God has promised to bless us, but He does not owe us anything because we are good.

The difference between poverty and riches in the kingdom of heaven is one of attitude. Paul wrote in Philippians 2:5, "Have this attitude in yourselves which was also in Christ Jesus...." Jesus' attitude was that He emptied Himself. James writes, warning the church of an attitude that considers a wealthy person to be of more value than the poor person.

> *For if a man comes into your assembly with a gold ring and dressed in fine clothes, and there also comes in a poor man in dirty clothes, and you pay special attention to the one who is wearing the fine clothes, and say, "You sit here in a good place," and you say to the poor man, "You stand over there, or sit down by my footstool," have you not made distinctions among yourselves, and become judges with evil motives?* (James 2:2-4)

I am afraid that the poor man would not even dare to enter many of our fancy buildings.

Jesus continues by telling them that they will be suffering more persecution. He is speaking to the end-time church when He says that it will last ten days. The period of ten days is not to be taken literally, but was a way of indicating that the time was finite and would be coming to an end. It is important for us to understand that the great tribulation of which Jesus spoke will eventually come to an end. Even though some die, we must not give up hope.

The key for understanding the tribulation is found in Revelation 12:11. Almost everyone that I have asked about this verse responds that we overcome Satan by the blood of the Lamb and the word of our testimony. Sometimes it comes as a surprise when I share with them the rest of the verse.

> *And they overcame him because of the blood of the Lamb and because of the word of their testimony, and* they did not love their life even to death (Revelation 12:11, emphasis added).

In warfare between nations, the objective is often to kill as many people as possible. It often is the case that victory belongs to the nation or people that kills the greatest number of the soldiers of the opposing army.

We must remember that it is Satan, not men, who is our enemy, and God's method of defeating Satan is different from ours. God has given us the weapons with which to defeat the enemy, and as Paul points out in I Corinthians 13, they are faith, hope, and love. We often get sentimental about this chapter, especially at weddings, but the reason love is the greatest is that the type of love that Paul is talking about here is *agape*—love that transcends life itself.

The theme of faith, hope, and love is repeated often, and it is in the verse quoted above as well. We appropriate the "blood of the Lamb" by faith, and we speak of the hope that is within us as our testimony. But it is the love that we have for Jesus that exceeds even our love of life itself that equips us to face the worst that Satan can throw against us.

It is interesting to note that at the time the apostles were writing their letters, they believed that Jesus was coming back very soon. While they were mistaken in the timing of His return, the result is that we have letters written to the church facing end-times situations. When we begin to look at these letters, and also much of the teaching of Jesus, in the light of the approaching end-times events, we begin to see them in a new light. I have been amazed as I have been reading the Gospels in the light of impending persecution.

As Jesus identifies Himself to this church, He says that He is the one who was dead and has come to life. It is Jesus, not Satan, who has the power over life and death. Satan may have the ability at times to kill our bodies, but that is not death. The death of the body is only temporary, not permanent. The death that is separation from God is eternal. As Jesus said,

> Do not fear those who kill the body but are unable to kill the soul; but rather fear him who is able to destroy both soul and body in hell (Matthew 10:28).

Those who have suffered physical persecution for the sake of Jesus seem to understand that verse. To kill the body is not death, it is victory. Polycarp did not fear the death of the body nearly as much as he loved Jesus. It is that kind of love that defeats Satan.

The focus of Jesus' letter to Smyrna is the answer to the question of what is victory. Death in the kingdom of heaven is not defeat; in fact, it is victory for the one who loves Jesus more than his own life. One day, if we are faithful and privileged to give our life for Jesus, we will be able to shout with Paul,

Death is swallowed up in victory. O death, where is your victory? O death, where is your sting? (I Corinthians 15:54-55).

As difficult as it is to see from our perspective, we have the victory now.

CHAPTER NOTES

[1] A Roman province in what is now Turkey.

[2] Barclay, William, *The Revelation of John, Vol. 1,* The Westminster Press (Philadelphia, PA), pp. 75-77.

CHAPTER 15

PERGAMUM—Servant Leadership

I will give you the crown of life (Revelation 2:10).

Pergamum was a very impressive city. It was described as a "royal city, the home of authority,"[1] as it sat on top of a huge hill, totally dominating the large plain that lay before it. Although it would never be an important commercial city, it was one of the great religious centers of the Greek world. Contained within it were two famous religious shrines—one a great altar to Zeus and the other to a god known as Asclepios Soter, or Asclepios the Savior.

Pergamum was also the administrative center for the Roman province of Asia, and as such was the center of Caesar worship. Caesar worship was particularly abhorrent to the Christian, since anyone who would not confess "Caesar is Lord" was subject to immediate death. Perhaps that is why Jesus identified it as the dwelling place of Satan.

The theme of Jesus' letter to Pergamum is contained in Hebrews 4:12.

> *For the word of God is living and active and sharper than any two-edged sword, and piercing as far as the division of soul and spirit, of both joints and*

*marrow, and able to judge the thoughts and inten-
tions of the heart.*

One of the things that John saw when he looked at
Jesus was that "out of His mouth came a sharp two-
edged sword" (Revelation 1:16), and this is the way in
which Jesus identified Himself to the church at
Pergamum. When used with skill, a double-edged sword
was a fiercesome weapon in Roman times because it was
able to cut equally well both forward and backward as it
was swung.

There is much confusion today concerning soul and
spirit, with both of these words often being used care-
lessly. Man is a triune being and is made up of body,
soul, and spirit. The body is the shell or dwelling place
for the soul and the spirit, and is not permanent. The
soul, consisting of the mind, will, and emotions, is that
part of our being with which we are most familiar.
Finally, the spirit is that part of us that God created man
with He said, "Let Us create man in Our image." It is
eternal and, since God is spirit, it is of the same nature
as God Himself.

It is our spirit that is reborn or comes alive when we
accept Jesus as our Lord and Savior. Our regenerated
spirit hears God speak and desires to walk in perfect
obedience and fellowship with Him. God's design for
mankind is that our body is the servant of the soul, and
the soul the servant of our spirit as our spirit is in submission to God. The problems that we face as we try to
walk with God are not in the realm of our spirit, but in
our soul.

Man's soul often rises up and seeks to dominate his
spirit, making it difficult for us to distinguish between
them. Paul uses the word "flesh" (*sarx* in the Greek) to

describe that part of the soul that refuses to obey the spirit. God's design is that each one would walk according to the direction of His spirit, not according to the desires of the soul. When we walk according to the soul, we often fall into the trap of walking in the flesh. Paul describes the tension between the spirit and the flesh as being like warfare (Galatians 5:16-17).

One of the things that the word of God does, acting in our lives as a two-edged sword, is that it separates what is spiritual from what is of the soul. The spirit can never be deceived, but it is easy for that to happen to the soul. That is why the soul cannot be trusted. It is too easy for us to rationalize fleshly behavior.

Not only do we as individuals sometimes walk soulishly, but we do it corporately in our churches as well. That was the situation with the church in Pergamum, and Jesus is going to bring His sword to bear in the life of this church. The same problems that Jesus identified in the Pergamum church pervade the end-times church today.

Jesus begins by commending them that in the past they were faithful in very trying and difficult circumstances. However, some problems with the church have developed over time. What has happened is that they have moved from being spiritual people—walking according to the things of the Spirit—to relying on the soul and walking in deception.

It is difficult to live among worldly and fleshly people without adopting some of their lifestyle. Jesus is critical that there are some among them "who hold to the teaching of Balaam." Balaam was a prophet during the time the children of Israel were moving from Egypt to the Promised Land. The problem with Balaam was not the way in which he prophesied. As much as he wanted to, he could not prophesy against the Israelites (see Numbers 22-23). Nevertheless, he did mix the holy with the profane. It was later that Balaam gave counsel to Israel. The counsel of Balaam was a compromise of the standards that God set, in that he taught that the men of Israel could take for themselves wives among the Moabites. (See Numbers 31:16.) The "teaching of Balaam" was that you could adopt worldly standards of behavior and still remain holy.

The second problem area that Jesus identified was that the church in Pergamum succumbed to the teaching of the "Nicolaitans." This is not the first time Jesus mentioned the Nicolaitans, since He commended the Ephesian church that they "hate the deeds of the Nicolaitans, which I also hate" (Revelation 2:6). It is not immediately apparent in our English translations who the Nicolaitans are. Some believe that the Nicolaitans were the followers of a man named Nicolas, who lived a profligate lifestyle, but it is highly unlikely in this context. Whoever they are, it is serious, since Jesus hates their deeds.

The most probable derivation of the term "nicolaitan" is that it is a combination of two Greek words: the first being *nikos* or *nicao*, which means to dominate or manipulate; the other word is *laos*, which means "the people" and is the word from which we derive the term laity. Taken together, a nicolaitan is one who dominates or uses the people to serve his own purposes.

One of the major problems in the church today is the distinction within the church between the clergy and laity. That distinction divides the people into two groups—the clergy in whom authority is vested and who, because of their titles and position, are often perceived to be better Christians than the rest and the laity, who are thus second-class citizens because they have not had formal training in theological matters.

Dr. Ken Blue, in his book *Healing Spiritual Abuse,* puts it this way:

> Ecclesiastical hierarchies...are founded on a sharp distinction between clergy and laity. The professional ministry (clergy) exists apart from the people (laity). The clergy play by different rules. They have different privileges, answer to a different set of expectations and are judged by different standards of conduct.
>
> The clergy are thought of as having privileged access to God's higher wisdom. While spiritual leaders protest such assumptions, their unspoken signals often contradict their words. The laity may indeed conduct activities labeled "ministry." But the real "ministry" is often ferociously defended and jealously guarded (p. 142).

Jesus specifically spoke to this issue when He said to His disciples,

> *You know that the rulers of the Gentiles lord it over them, and their great men exercise authority over them. It is not so among you, but whoever wishes to become great among you shall be your slave; just as the Son of Man did not come to be served, but to serve, and to give His life a ransom for many* (Matthew 20:25-28)

It is sad that so many in positions of church leadership are motivated by having their needs met by those whom they watch over. Harry Jackson, speaking at the Mid-Atlantic Leadership Conference in Lancaster, Pennsylvania, said it this way:

101

> You see ministry and God's message as a way of fulfilling your ego needs. Instead of meeting with God, you are trying to be somebody in God. You are trying to build a kingdom, not trying to respond to the King of the Kingdom.

This sounds a lot like the evil slaves in the parable Jesus told. Many of us do not understand our true motivations. In Jeremiah 16:19-17:18, God speaks through the prophet,

> The heart [i.e. motivation] is more deceitful than all else and is desperately sick; I, the Lord, search the heart, I test the mind, Even to give to each man according to his ways, According to the results of his deeds (Jeremiah 17:9-10).

According to Ephesians 4:11, the purpose of leadership within the church is to be servants of the people that the people, the saints, may be trained and equipped to do the work of the ministry. It is the privilege of every believer, everyone who is born again of the Spirit, to be able to hear God and receive revelation from Him. Each saint has a calling, a part to fulfill in the body of Christ, that is unique to him, yet relatively few saints could tell you what their calling is.

One of the tragic stories in the Old Testament is related in Exodus 19 and 20 and occurs soon after the children of Israel left Egypt. Moses brought the children of Israel to the foot of the mountain, and God instructed Moses that He was going to meet with the people on the third day and what they needed to do to prepare. A wonderful thing was going to happen. Instead of just speaking to one man, Moses, God was going to speak directly to the people. However, the people became frightened and said to Moses, "Speak to us yourself and we will listen; but let not God speak to us, lest we die" (Exodus 20:19).

Each man and woman had the opportunity to hear God speaking directly to them, yet they were afraid of the responsibility. Instead they told Moses that he should hear God and then tell them what God said. That is the pattern of the Old Testament. A few chosen ones, i.e. the prophets, heard God and told the people what God said.

But it was to be different in the New Testament, because every person that received Jesus came alive in the spirit and could now hear God themselves. Revelation from God was not the domain of a few gifted ones, as it was in the Old Testament times, but now belonged to the entire body.

There was a wonderful example of how this can operate in the body that I heard of recently. During the last several years, I have ministered at a fellowship in the rural city of Solwezi, Zambia. Recently, some fellow saints, Brenda and Eric Kniss, were ministering there on the subject of hearing God. During a recess, Brenda, who was the session leader, suggested that instead of fellowshipping with each other they go apart and hear what God was saying to them. It was immediately apparent that each person took that seriously as they scattered to find their own places.

When they came back together again, the people were excited. It seemed the pastors and elders, who were sitting towards the front wanted to share first, but Brenda asked them to wait. Instead she started with the women towards the back and then some of the men who were not church leaders. As each one shared what God spoke to him/her, Eric made notes. After some time they paused, and Eric organized what the people had shared. He then repeated back to them what God had been saying. Brenda then turned to the pastors and elders and asked if this was what God had been showing them. They were surprised because these things were exactly what they were hearing from God.

Many people who come to church every Sunday morning have little experience in hearing and understanding God because they have been told that is the job of the preacher. On the other hand, many pastors are afraid to trust the people. In many church buildings the pastor is positioned high above the people, which is often symbolic of how they picture themselves spiritually.

Properly functioning leadership will help believers to become mature in the faith, to hear the voice of Jesus clearly, to know their spiritual calling and giftings, and will therefore train them in the work of ministry to others. That takes more than hearing the pastor deliver a sermon on Sunday morning or watching a well known speaker on television. Paul wrote that Jesus has appointed apostles, prophets, evangelists, shepherds, and teachers, who working together can equip the saints so that they, the saints, can do the work of ministry.

Like the church at Pergamum, we need to seek God and have Him reveal the ways in which we are nicolaitans. We need to repent and allow the sword of the word of God, the living and active word, to be wielded by Jesus.

So many in the ministry are afraid that if they were to become servant leaders and give up their big programs with their large attendance, that the cost will be too high and they will lose too much. Yet the promise that Jesus made to the church at Pergamum was that He would provide everything they needed. However, He would do it in a supernatural and hidden way, so that "no one knows but he who receives it."

For the one who repents and overcomes, the reward will come in three parts. First of these was "some of the hidden manna." As the children of Israel were wandering in the wilderness following their deliverance from Egypt, God supernaturally supplied them with a bread-like substance they called manna. It was food directly from the hand of God and had to be collected fresh every day. There is also a source of hidden manna.

When Jesus was ministering to the Samaritan woman at the well, as recorded in John 4, there is no record that He had anything to eat. When the disciples returned they remarked to Jesus that He had had nothing to eat. His response was that He had food to eat that they did not know about, and that His food was to do the work of His Father. Likewise, the promise here is that for the one who will put away the things of the flesh and rely on things of the Spirit, God will supernaturally supply his needs.

Secondly, the overcomer is promised a "white stone," which in Roman times represented approval. "The white stone was a symbol in the Roman world used in legal trials, academic grading systems, and at athletic games. The stone with the Roman letters SP printed upon it was given in Roman games as an award for valor."[2]

Finally the overcomer is granted a new name written on the stone, which speaks of a new identity. "It was also first-century practice that after a serious illness a patient who recovered would often take a new name to signify his or her complete recovery."3 This new identity is not apparent to everyone, but is hidden in Jesus.

CHAPTER NOTES

[1] Sir William Ramsay, as quoted in Barclay, op. cit., p.87.

[2] Palmer, Earl F., *The Communicator's Commentary: 1, 2, 3 John, Revelation*, Lloyd J. Ogilvie, ed., Word Books (1982), p. 138.

[3] Ibid., p. 138.

CHAPTER 16

THYATIRA—Submissive Authority

I will give you the crown of life (Revelation 2:10).

Thyatira was perhaps the least important of the seven cities to which the letters were directed. It was a great commercial city, since it lay on the road between Pergamum, the capital of Asia, and Sardis, a road that was crowded with the commerce of Asia and the east.

However, the city was unimportant religiously, and there was relatively little persecution of the church in Thyatira. The only other mention of Thyatira in the Bible is that Lydia, a seller of purple fabric who responded to the message spoken by Paul, lived there.

In this letter to Thyatira, Jesus presented Himself as the one who brings judgment in the church. In Revelation 1, Jesus is described as having eyes that "were like a flame of fire" (v.15) and feet that "were like burnished bronze, when it has been made to glow in a furnace" (v.16), which is the same description that He gives of Himself in this letter. Both fire and bronze are symbolic of judgment. For example, in the Tabernacle, the Altar of Sacrifice was made of acacia wood covered with bronze, and it was on that altar that sacrifices were made for sin and transgression.

Jesus first commends the church at Thyatira, not only on their deeds, but also on their love, faith, service, and perseverance. Yet there is a problem upon which He brings correction and judgment. They have permitted a woman identified as Jezebel or like Jezebel who "leads My bondservants astray."

In the Old Testament, Jezebel was the wife of Ahab, the ninth king of Israel and the daughter of the Phoenician king of Tyre and Sidon. When she became Ahab's wife, she brought with her the worship of Philistine gods, Baal and Asherah, and led the entire nation into idolatry and apostasy. Under her orders the prophets of God were slain, and it was only through the faithfulness of Obadiah, the head of the king's household, that 100 of them were saved. She also attempted to kill Elijah after he defeated and killed the 400 prophets of Baal (I King 18, 19). The worst thing, in this context, that Jezebel did was that she usurped the role of her husband, and this behavior extended towards her son as well.

This person in the church at Thyatira did similar things. Calling herself a prophetess, this one called "Jezebel" used her influence to lead believers into immorality and refused to be in submission to those whom God had raised up as leaders. Exercising unlawful authority is called usurpation. She took bondservants of Jesus and caused them to be unfaithful to the One to Whom they belonged. There is no doubt, since she had no desire to repent, that she did so willingly.

Many churches have been severely damaged because of those who usurp authority and refuse to submit. Submission in the church and in the family is often misunderstood. First of all, submission in the church is voluntary. One cannot come and demand that we obey them, for that kind of obedience is servitude. God's instruction is that we are to "obey [our] leaders, and submit to them" (Hebrews 13:17), not because they wield power but because they are the ones appointed by Jesus to "watch over our souls."

Secondly, submission is active. Many of us get upset when we are going through a difficult time and the pastor does not come to visit. It is quite possible that the pastor does not even know we are having troubles. It is really up to us to take the initiative and seek help.

Finally, those to whom we are submitted "watch over our souls," not our spirits. In other words, their job is not to be god to us, that is, to tell us what God wants us to do. It is the responsibility of each believer to hear God for himself. Their primary responsibility is the well-being of our souls—our thought life, emotional being, and how we make decisions.

From the perspective of the Church undergoing tribulation, the real problem with rebellious behavior is that it brings about disunity. Disunity within the Church is a serious problem, especially during times of persecution. It brings about division and weakness, and a "house divided against itself will not stand" (Matthew 12:25). When the church is suffering tribulation, disunity causes the saints to be exposed to unnecessary danger.

Unity within the church is not the same as unity in worldly organizations. That is because the church is not an organization, but more like a family. Unity is not everyone believing exactly the same thing, but rather unity in the church is like unity in the family—it is built on relationship, trust, and respect. In this context, authority is not based on title, position, or strength; it is earned through service and is expressed through honor.

Unity begins with an attitude of serving Jesus as the Head of the church, and recognizing that Jesus has placed gifts of service, ministry gifts, within each saint. These are not natural "talents" that the world recognizes and uses as the basis for hierarchy. They are supernatural "grace gifts" that enable each saint to do the work that Jesus has called them to do. Apostle, prophet, evangelist, shepherd, and teacher are some gifts, but there are many others. As we submit to Jesus as our Head, we also recognize and submit to the gifting that He has placed in each of our brothers and sisters in the Lord. No gifting from God is superior to another, so we do not lord it over one another. Rather we let the gift of Christ in us express itself in service, doing so in a way that brings honor and respect.

Jesus warns the church that He is not going to allow this situation to occur much longer and calls for those who are involved to repent. It is interesting to note that of all the corrective measures that are mentioned in the New Testament, this is one of the most severe. Very early in the life of the church, a similarly severe judgment was demonstrated when two people attempted to deceive everyone. The story of Ananias and Sapphira is found in Acts 5:1-13, and the result of God's judgment on them was that the church was held in high esteem. There will be a similar result in the latter day church when "all the churches will know that I am He who searches the minds and hearts" (Revelation 2:23).

The reward for those who are faithful to walk in proper submission is authority. There is a fascinating encounter between Jesus and a Roman centurion that is recounted in Luke 7:1-10. When word reaches the centurion that Jesus has turned aside and is coming to heal his servant he sends word to Jesus.

Just say the word, and my servant will be healed. For indeed, I am a man under authority, with sol- diers under me; and I say to this one, "Go!" and he goes; and to another, "Come!" and he comes; and to my slave, "Do this!" and he does it (Luke 7:7-8).

Luke records that when Jesus heard this statement, He was astonished. Using his military experience, the centurion clearly annunciated the principle of authority: to have authority you must be under authority. That au- thority, however, is not unlimited, but works only within bounds set by the relationships of the people both above and below in the chain.

A similar principle applied in the life of Jesus. In His earthly ministry, Jesus always walked in perfect submis- sion to His Father. The gospels give witness that He only did what He saw His Father doing, and He only said the things that He heard His Father say. The essence of sin is disobedience, and never did Jesus sin. Because of His perfect submission, including submitting to the horrors and humiliation of the crucifixion, Jesus was able to say that all authority in heaven and on the earth was given to Him.

Several years ago I was ministering in South Africa in a home meeting. I was sitting across the circle from the leader, who was talking on the subject of wives being submitted to their own husbands (Ephesians 5:22). There were two women seated next to him, and as he began talking, I could see the negative reaction on their faces. It was like the hair stood up on the back of their necks. God showed me that the reason these women re- acted the way they did was that they did not see their husbands in submission to anyone.

How can we say that we are in submission to Jesus

and not be in submission to the one whom He has placed in our lives? In the case of the centurion, he could not say he was serving Caesar if he did not obey legitimate orders from his own superior officer, who represented Caesar.

The reward for submission is authority, and this authority comes from God alone. Authority is not how loud we speak, but the effect of the words we say and the things we do. For example, there is no indication in the Gospels that Jesus had to shout and harangue demons to come out. He simply spoke in the authority that was His.

Many churches in America today have been greatly weakened because of people like the Jezebel in Thyatira. The promise of this letter is that there is coming a time when He is not going to let it continue. It is His church, and He is going to watch over it.

CHAPTER 17

SARDIS—Hopeful Watching

Wake up... (Revelation 3:2).

S ardis had once been a great and powerful city. At the time that Jesus dictated this letter to the church there, however, it had fallen into degeneration. Many years before, Cyrus, king of Persia, had initiated a siege of the city, which sat on the top of a steep hill and was virtually impregnable. However, one of Cyrus' soldiers found a way up the cliff through a large crack in the rock, and in the middle of the night he led a party of Persian troops up the crack. When they arrived at the top, they found the battlements unprotected. The Sardinians believed themselves to be so well protected that they did not even post a guard.

In 17 A.D. Sardis was destroyed by an earthquake, but was rebuilt through the financial largesse of the Roman emperor. It was again wealthy, but there was no life or spirit there.[1] That apparently was the situation with the church there as well.

The opening of the letter to Sardis is rather simple. Jesus is identified as the One "who has the seven Spirits of God, and the seven stars." The reference to the seven stars goes back to the appearance of Jesus in chapter 1. John saw Him holding seven stars in His right hand (v. 16) as He stood among the seven lampstands. Jesus then told John that the seven stars represent the "angels of the seven churches." The word translated as angel literally means a messenger, and in this context probably represent the messengers to the churches. That they are in His right hand indicates that they are His messengers. The church is not only the possession of Jesus, it is the very presence of Christ in the earth.

Jesus also has the "seven Spirits of God," which requires a little explanation. There are three additional references to the seven Spirits of God in the book of Revelation: 1:4, 4:5 and 5:6. In chapter 4 the seven Spirits of God are described as "seven lamps of fire burning before the throne." Then in chapter 5 we have a picture of Jesus as the Lamb "as if slain" (v. 6). There is a feature of this Lamb that is unusual. He has "seven horns and seven eyes, which are the seven Spirits of God, sent out into all the earth."

It is important to realize that there is only one Holy Spirit, as Paul states emphatically in Ephesians 4:4-6. The fact that there are seven of everything—seven lamps, seven horns, seven eyes and seven spirits—would indicate that the number seven is important. Seven is understood to be the number of completion. For example, when God created the heavens and the earth He did so in seven days.[2] So whatever the lamps, horns, eyes, and spirits represent, they are complete.

Recall that this book was written as a letter to the "seven churches that are in Asia." Certainly it is true that there is only one church, the Body of Christ, just as it is true that there is but one Holy Spirit. In terms of the prophetic context of this book the significance of seven churches is two-fold. First, they represent the entire church; and secondly, the church is being brought to completion.

Revelation is an account of God bringing everything to completion. Everything that was destroyed by Satan in the garden is being restored. As lamps represent the revelation of God, the revelation of Jesus is going to be complete in the earth. As horns represent power and government, the government of God is being perfectly established. As eyes represent knowledge, the knowledge of God will be known be every person. Finally, as the seven Spirits move into all the earth, the job of the Holy Spirit to convict of sin and draw men to Jesus will have been completed. As Paul says in I Corinthians 13:9-12,

For we know in part, and we prophesy [revelation] in part; but when the perfect [complete] comes, the partial will be done away. When I was a child, I used to think as a child, reason as a child; when I became a man, I did away with childish things. For now we see in a mirror dimly, but then face to face; now I know in part, but then I shall know fully just as I also have been fully known.

This church is in serious trouble. Jesus said to them that they think they are alive, but, in fact, they are dead. God was busy at work bringing His purposes for creation to completion, and they were totally unaware of what was happening. This end-time church is asleep, deceived into thinking that nothing unusual was happening in the world. It was like the ancient city of Sardis was deceived when they believed their fortress was impregnable, and they slept instead of being watchful.

In some ways a church is like a city; it is a community of believers, and within that community, God has placed people with various jobs and responsibilities. One of those jobs is the watchman on the wall. The sole responsibility of the watchman is to stand on the wall and look as far into the distance as he can for any telltale signs that the enemy might be approaching. If he sees the enemy coming, he is to warn the leadership.

In Ezekiel 33 God instructs us about being watchmen. He points out that if the watchman sounds the alarm and the city decides to ignore it, then he is absolved of any responsibility for the fate of the city. If, however, he fails to give the alarm, then the blood of all those in the city who perish as a result is upon his head.

Deception is a serious trap in which to fall. Many are deceived today into believing that there is nothing wrong. Some are not sounding the warning when the signs are clearly there. Others are choosing to ignore the warnings that are being broadcast. Peter warns that just about the time they are comfortable in their thinking, judgment will fall upon them with terrifying fire (II Peter 3:3-7). Likewise, Jesus warns Sardis that unless they wake up He is going to come upon them like a thief in the night.

The church in Sardis may have been dead, but that does not mean that it was without hope. Jesus is the one who resurrects people from the dead, and He issues a command to the church to "Wake up!" It is not unlike when Jesus stood before the tomb of Lazarus and called, "Lazarus, come forth!" All Lazarus' friends and family were standing around weeping and wailing, but Jesus spoke the words of hope.

We must never think for a moment that there is no hope. Our job is to rekindle hope where there seems to be none. When people lose hope, they also lose the ability to change. Although there is going to come a day when hope will disappear, and it "will come like a thief," until that day there is always the possibility for change.

Notice also Jesus' emphasis on deeds: "for I have not found your deeds completed in the sight of My God." It is not enough for us simply to "go to church." Even though they would not admit it, there are many who have the attitude that they are somehow doing God a favor by showing up on Sunday morning. Jesus has called us to be servants, bondservants. It is not enough for us, like Little Jack Horner, to sit in our corner and say, "What a good boy am I."

While it is true that we do not earn our salvation by the deeds we do, that salvation is a free gift from God, consider these scriptures:

Let your light shine before men in such a way that they may see your good works, and glorify your Father who is in heaven. (Matthew 5:16)

For we are His workmanship, created in Christ Jesus for good works, which God prepared beforehand, that we should walk in them. (Ephesians 2:10)

Looking for the blessed hope and the appearing of the glory of our great God and Savior, Christ Jesus; who gave Himself for us, that He might redeem us from every lawless deed and purify for Himself a people for His own possession, zealous for good deeds (Titus 2:13-14).

Let us hold fast the confession of our hope without wavering, for He who promised is faithful; and let us consider how to stimulate one another to love and good deeds (Hebrews 10:23-24).

We are called to be bond-slaves of Jesus. A bondservant is one who enters into a master/slave relationship willingly, out of gratitude and love for the master, and a good bondservant does the will of his master first. "Good deeds" are those things that are the will of the master. Some good deeds are general to all, such as "making disciples of all nations," while others are specific to individuals. (See I Corinthians 12:14-31.) What brings death to a church is when we decide to do what we want to do, which quickly degenerates into empty ritual.

Even in Sardis there are a few people who have not succumbed to deadness around them. In the midst of apathy and lack of life, Jesus recognizes those who still have life, and He encourages them. As Elijah discovered in the midst of an apostate nation, God never leaves Himself without a remnant.

The reward pronounced for those overcomers in Sardis is one of the most magnificent promises of the Bible: "I will confess his name before My Father, and before His angels." What a great motivation this has been to myriads of saints over hundreds of years.

The picture that this phrase evokes is that of Stephen as he was being stoned. Stephen was the first martyr of the church, and as the people gathered around him to begin hurling stones at him, he spoke, and said, "Behold, I see the heavens opened up and the Son of Man standing at the right hand of God" (Acts 7:56). This is truly remarkable, for according to the testimony of Paul, Jesus is seated at God's right hand. Now Jesus is witnessing the faithfulness of His servant, Stephen, and stands out of respect. I would not be surprised if Jesus was confessing to His Father. "See, Father. That is Stephen! He is one of Mine."

It is a great disservice that the Church does when it does not teach the coming of Jesus and the promises of God that will be fulfilled in the last days. When things get difficult and persecution comes, it is the hope instilled by this promise, and others like it, that sustains and strengthens.

CHAPTER NOTES

[1] Barclay, op. cit., pp. 113-115.

[2] It was on the seventh day that God created rest. He did not rest because He was tired, but rather He created rest for our benefit. The seventh day, being a day of rest, also represents that He was finished with creation; it was completed.

CHAPTER 18

PHILADELPHIA—
Supernatural Power

*I will keep you from the hour
of testing...* (Revelation 3:10).

P hiladelphia, which in Greek literally means the
one who loves his brother, was the youngest of
the seven cities. When Philadelphia was founded
its purpose was that it would be a center for promoting
the Greek language and culture to the surrounding
areas. Now the church in Philadelphia had the mission
of carrying the message of the love of God in Christ
Jesus.

When Jesus greeted the church in Philadelphia, He
identified Himself as the One who "has the key of David,
who opens and no one will shut, and who shuts and no
one opens." Throughout the book of Revelation there
are several mentions of keys, but the reference here to
the key of David is taken directly from the prophet
Isaiah.

> *And I will clothe him with your tunic, And tie your
> sash securely about him, I will entrust him with your
> authority, And he will become a father to the inhabi-
> tants of Jerusalem and to the house of Judah. Then I
> will set the key of the house of David on his shoulder,
> When he opens no one will shut, When he shuts no*

one will open. And I will drive him like a peg in a firm place, And he will become a throne of glory to his father's house (Isaiah 22:21-23).

The context of this fascinating prophecy concerns one named Shebna, who is supposed to be the steward of the royal household of King David. A steward is one who holds or maintains something on behalf of the owner, but Shebna has apparently usurped the place of the owner instead. He has assumed for himself a position of authority to which he was not entitled; and since he was steward of the royal household, it is obvious he has assumed the position of the king. God speaks quite harshly to him, saying that "He is about to hurl you headlong, O man."

Jesus' reference to this prophecy in this context and His assertion that He is the one who holds the key of David would indicate that Shebna is symbolic of someone or something throughout the churches. In Ephesians 2:19 Paul identifies that we in the church are a part of God's household. Thus the men that Jesus has placed in positions of leadership are in the position of being His stewards. This is very much like the situation described by Jesus in the parable of the wise and evil slaves. Like the evil slaves in that parable, some of these men have taken upon themselves the mantle of Jesus Himself and have usurped His authority. Peter is clear that in the days leading up to the return of Jesus that judgment will "begin with the household of God" (I Peter 4:17).

Large ecclesiastical organizations tend to draw people to themselves, and some of the leaders of these organizations have been guilty. However, there are also many whom Jesus has entrusted with part, even a small part, of His household and given a position of leadership, who then have attempted to become as Jesus to the people, ruling them according to their own manmade laws and regulations.

As with the letter to Pergamum, it is important to distinguish between spirit and soul. Our spirit is that part of us created in the image of God and is of the same nature as His nature. No one but Jesus has authority over another man's spirit. The writer of Hebrews states it is the position of leadership in the church to "keep watch over your souls," (Hebrews 13:17) that is, your well being. Any man who claims to hear God on behalf of another is assuming the place of Jesus. The purpose of prophecy, especially personal prophecy, and indeed all of the grace gifts, is to build up, exhort, and strengthen, not to rule.

Within the church, leaders are not to exercise authority over those entrusted to them. It is the responsibility of believers to submit to their leaders, who in turn serve them. Jesus taught His disciples that leadership in the body of Christ is not exercised through authority like "the rulers of the Gentiles," but through servanthood (see Matthew 20:24-28). Jesus went so far as to illustrate the principle of servant leadership when He became the lowliest of all servants in the household and washed the feet of the disciples.

Apparently, there is no such problem within the church in Philadelphia, for like the church in Smyrna, Jesus has nothing negative to say to this church. He then goes on to tell them that He has set before them "an open door which no one can shut."

While we often speak of an "open door of opportunity," this use of open door has to do with spiritual matters. It is a clear reference to Jesus announcing that He is the one who holds the key of David; that is, Jesus is the rightful head of God's household and is the only one entitled to sit on the throne of David. Jesus is the one to whom all authority was given.

As the church walks in submission to Jesus, He does grant it authority in heavenly places. We do not have authority over one another in the church, but we do have a measure of authority over the enemy. In the name of Jesus we have authority over evil spirits, the demons, and to some small measure over Satan himself. We also have authority in the name of Jesus over the works of the enemy, such as sickness and disease.

Jesus commends this church that, although they do not have much power in a human sense, they do walk in the authority of Jesus over the enemy. As the church we can only walk at the level of authority that He grants, not that we desire, and because this church walked in humility before Him, Jesus says that He is going to increase that authority so that even those who serve Satan will come to recognize it.

There is an interesting contrast between how Jesus encourages the churches in Philadelphia and Smyrna. While the believers in Smyrna are warned that they will face suffering and tribulation, but they are to be faithful, the believers in Philadelphia are told that they will be kept "from the hour of testing, that hour which is about to come upon the whole world." That is, by some supernatural means Jesus is going to protect this church from the tribulation that will devastate so much of the church world-wide. We can take that to mean that there will be some churches that will escape the tribulation, not by being removed, but by being protected in the heavens.

Some have suggested that, although Jesus had

nothing negative to speak of the church in Smyrna, the fact that they would face tribulation is an indication that something is not quite what it should be. They state that there must be some hidden sin. However, that conclusion falls under the category of the doctrine of demons. Those who put forth this idea fall into the same trap that the friends of Job did. Job's friends assumed that his trials were a result of something bad he did. In fact they occurred because he was righteous, and God allowed Satan to test him to prove that his righteousness was genuine.

God clearly has a purpose in allowing the church in Philadelphia to escape tribulation. It demonstrates His supernatural power over the power of the enemy. He also has a purpose in allowing the church in Smyrna to suffer tribulation. It also demonstrates His supernatural power over the power of the enemy as it works through the lives of faithful believers. When believers are subjected to all the tribulation that the enemy can throw at them and they still remain faithful and glorify God, it goes far beyond the natural ability of man to the supernatural.

What is true in the church is also true in the life of individuals. We must never conclude that because a believer is being tested by the enemy that it is a sign that he is somehow unspiritual or has sinned in some way. Such a belief can be categorized as a doctrine of demons.

The seat of government, and thus authority, for King David was Jerusalem. The seat of government for the new Millennial Kingdom will also be Jerusalem, restored after the ravages of the final battle of Armageddon. Likewise, the seat of government when Satan is permanently thrown into the lake of fire and brimstone and God creates the new heaven and new earth (Revelation 21) will be the new Jerusalem.

The reward for those who walk in humble obedience before Jesus will be that they are permanently at home in the seat of power of the Kingdom of God.

There is a purpose for the church. Being faithful in the last days is not just a matter that we somehow simply survive. That is a passive approach. Being an overcomer requires an active, even aggressive, approach to life. Jesus promised the end-time church of Philadelphia that He would open a door that no one can shut. That implies the willingness on the part of the believers to walk through it to accomplish some purpose.

CHAPTER 19

LAODICEA—Overcoming Process

You are neither cold nor hot... (Revelation 3:16).

Laodicea was an important financial and commercial center in Asia. It lay astride the great road that stretched from the port of Ephesus and stretched eastward into Syria. Without peace, there is not prosperity, and when the Romans conquered Asia they brought peace. As a result Laodicea flourished, and the wealth in Laodicea was enormous. It was a major banking and financial center, a center for the manufacture of clothing, and it even had a major medical school. In addition, the city contained a very large Jewish community estimated as being at least 7,500 Jewish males alone.[1]

From this and from some of the things Jesus said about the church in Laodicea, we can conclude that the Christians there were wealthy, as well. This stands in sharp contrast to the church in Smyrna and many other places where they were suffering persecution.

In the opening to this letter, Jesus identified Himself in three ways. First, He said that He is the Amen, which literally means "truly." It is used to affirm that what has just been said is truth, so for Jesus to identify Himself in this way is affirming that He is truth. In the western way of thinking, we tend to identify truth as facts, something that is objective and not dependent upon the one who said it. But from the biblical perspective, truth is tied to the one who has spoken. Truth is a person and has a name—Jesus. If something is not consistent with the nature of Jesus' person, then it is not truth. That means, for example, if one were to tell a lie, that is, an untruth, then he would be denying Jesus.

Secondly, Jesus says that He is the "faithful and true Witness." A witness, of course, is someone who was personally present at an event and observed it. In a court of law, attorneys will sometimes attempt to nullify the testimony of a witness by impeaching his character. If his character can be shown to be suspect, then his testimony may not to be counted for much. Jesus told His disciples that if they had seen Him, they had seen the Father, and that His character and behavior was a perfect reflection of God the Father. Many have attempted to find a flaw, even the slightest one, in Jesus but have been unable to do so.

Finally, Jesus says that He is the "Beginning of the creation of God." The NASB has a footnote concerning the word "beginning" (*arche* in the Greek), indicating that an alternate translation could be origin or source. So one could read this as Jesus is "the source of all the creation of God," and thus He is the source of everything we have and need. Paul wrote in his letter to the Colossians that "by Him all things were created...all things have been created by Him and for Him." (Colossians 1:16)

How Jesus identified Himself here is important in a legal sense, for He is about to put forth a stinging indictment. He stated that as the source of creation, He has the legal standing to make such an indictment; that what He is about to say is true; and that He is trustworthy and accurate. His indictment of Laodicea is in two parts.

In the first part Jesus says that the church in Laodicea is lukewarm. It is like taking a sip of coffee or tea expecting it to be hot, but finding it to be tepid. His reaction was to want to spit it out.

Spiritually, lukewarmness comes from an attitude that we are good enough and are satisfied with a certain level of religiousness. For example, if we just go to church once in a while or serve on a committee then that satisfies our religious duties.

The second part of the indictment is that they think they are rich and do not lack anything; when, in fact, they are poor and lack everything. The difference is their perspective compared to God's perspective.

There was a young man who came to Jesus and asked Him what he needed to do to receive eternal life. Jesus answered by listing six of the Ten Commandments given to Moses. When the young man answered that he had kept all of these, Jesus continued by telling the man to sell everything he had, give it to the poor, and follow Him. The Bible says that "he went away grieved, for he was one who owned much property."[2]

One of the difficulties with being wealthy is that we substitute reliance on God with reliance on our wealth. In the wealthy nations of the west, most of us would deny that we worship idols. After all, we think, that is what the Hindus do in India. An idol is not necessarily made of wood or stone; it is whatever we worship and obey, whatever we owe first allegiance. When the young man could not sell what he had, it was because his wealth as measured by lands and property was more important than eternal life. He never doubted what Jesus said; he just could not do it.

Often we say with our words that Jesus is Lord, but then turn around and behave as if money is lord. Look at the contrast between deeds and words. The Laodicean church says, "Look at what I say." Jesus says, "I know your deeds." How many times do our words and actions contradict one another? The young man said he obeyed the Law of Moses, but when he received the commandment of God he was unwilling to obey it.

Confessing one thing but doing the opposite is exactly the definition of the double minded man of which James speaks. We think we are asking in faith, but we first look at our checkbooks and balance sheets. God speaks, but we do not hear because our wallets are too thick, and they muffle the voice of God.

This indictment of Jesus speaks especially strongly to the wealthy churches of America. We have become a people who are obsessed with what God can do for us. What we do not realize is that God can remove our wealth in an instant. In the stock market crash of 1929, many fortunes were lost literally overnight, and some people committed suicide because they could not face the loss of their security. I wonder if that were to happen today, how many of those who jump would be Christians.

So the church in wealthy Laodicea stands indicted before God. Jesus, however, does not desire to spit anyone out of His mouth, so He speaks directly to the problem. He says, "I advise you to buy from Me gold refined by fire...and white garments, that you may cloth yourself...and eyesalve to anoint your eyes, that you may see" (Revelation 3:18).

The gold refined by fire represents the convicting work of the Holy Spirit to separate the dross, i.e. that which is of the flesh, from the metal, i.e. the things that are of God. This requires true repentance, which is agreeing with God that He is right and that we need to change. Once the dross is removed from the pure metal, it does not return. Repentance that does not bring about deep, long lasting change is not true repentance.

White garments speak of how we live, walking in purity of purpose. It is not obeying a set of moral laws that brings about purity, for unless the heart and motivations are changed, obeying a set of external laws does nothing. We need to bring our confession and deeds into alignment.

The eyesalve allows us to see the truth and receive revelation. The flesh does not want to hear from God; it is perfectly satisfied with the status quo. In fact, it really enjoys religious practices and does not see the necessity of hearing God. When our spiritual eyes are opened and our sight restored, we begin to see the things of God clearly.

The fruit of repentance for the Laodicean church is coming into a whole new level of intimacy with Jesus. In Revelation 3:20 the whole tone of the voice of Jesus changes from one of discipline to one of gentleness. He says that He is standing at the door of our heart, but on the outside.

Our heart is the seat of everything that is important to us. It involves our motivations, which in the realm of the natural we do not understand most of the time. Jeremiah says, "The heart is more deceitful than all else and is desperately sick" (Jeremiah 17:9). Perhaps that is why, when Paul prayed on behalf of the Ephesian church (and by extension us), he prayed that "the eyes of your heart may be enlightened" (Ephesians 1:18).

Many of us say that we have invited Jesus into our heart, yet for those in the Laodicean church He does not live there. That is why He is standing on the outside, knocking at the door. It is not simply that He comes through that door once for a little while. He comes in to live, to have supper with us.

It is interesting that Revelation 3:20 is quoted so often as an invitation to sinners to come to Jesus and receive Him as Lord. The context of this verse, however, is that Jesus is speaking to lukewarm believers. It is really an invitation to each believer to take open the door and fellowship with Jesus. How many times have we had an evening with good friends, where we sat around the table and talked? There is something special about sharing a meal with friends, and that is the way Jesus wants to be with us.

Jesus is not a distant, superior being who sits in heaven just waiting for us to make a mistake. He is a friend and a brother who seeks to share in the good and the difficult. It is incredible to think that the One who is the Amen and the Ruler of all Creation comes and dwells in each of us and fellowships with us.

In the light of the type of relationship that Jesus seeks to have with each of us, the reward for the overcomer in Laodicea is a favored position in the kingdom. The reward is for all those who overcome in the same manner and degree that Jesus overcame.

Near the end of Jesus' earthly ministry the mother of James and John approached Jesus and asked Him for a favor.[3] She desired that they be given special status when Jesus came into His kingdom by placing them to the right and left of the throne. In response to that request, Jesus asked if they were able to "drink of the cup that I am about to drink." He then pointed out that such a position was not His to grant, since "it is for those for whom it has been prepared by My Father."

The drinking of the cup to which Jesus was referring in this passage occurred a short time later in the Garden of Gethsemane. In total obedience and submission to His Father, He withstood the onslaught of Satan, even to the point of sweating drops of blood. I believe that the cup Jesus referred to in His prayer to His Father in the garden was not the impending death on the cross, because that was His purpose in coming. Rather, it was the tribulation that He was experiencing there, in the Garden of Gethsemane. For if He was unable to endure the full wrath of Satan in His body and soul, He would never make it to the cross.

When we walk through a forest and look at the trees, almost all of them look strong and sturdy. Yet, after the big storm comes, the hurricane with 125 mph winds, only the truly strong trees with deep roots are still standing. Those are the ones that have borne the full fury and brunt of the storm.

There are going to be some in the church who, during the great tribulation, will experience the total force that the enemy can bring to bear. Some are going to fall, but others will stand. They may be battered and broken, but they will still be standing. They will stand because the depth of their love for Jesus will anchor them in the storm.

That is the way that Jesus overcame, and His reward was to sit down with His Father in His throne. Likewise for those who face the fury of the Antichrist, yet remain obedient and submissive to Jesus.

CHAPTER NOTES

[1] Barclay, op. cit., pp 138-139

[2] This incident is found in Matthew 19:16-29; Mark 10:17-30 and Luke 18:18-30.

[3] See Matthew 20:20-23.

CHAPTER 20

The Church Fabric

*Choose for yourselves today whom
you will serve* (Joshua 24:15).

As he approached the end of his life, Joshua re-
flected on all that he had seen God do. Joshua
had served as one of Moses' lieutenants and pro-
tegés, and when Moses was taken to be with the Lord,
Joshua became the leader of the children of Israel. He
led them across the Jordan River into the Promised
Land. He experienced many terrific victories and made
a few mistakes. But now, like Moses, he was going to
leave the responsibility to others.

Joshua knew that there was one more thing he had
to do. Having led Israel for many years through victory
and defeat as the children of Israel occupied the land of
Canaan, which God had promised to Abraham, he called
the people together to make a decision. He knew that
there would be difficult times ahead for the young nation, and it was important that the people make a declaration now.

As an experienced and able leader, Joshua put it to
the people in a clear way. He first spoke the word of the
Lord to them, recounting to them how God had dealt
with them. They started as a group of individuals with a
common lineage,living as slaves in Egypt, and God

forged them into a people and a nation. He reminded the people of what God had done in their midst.

Then he presented them with a challenge. They could either serve the Lord God or they could serve foreign gods. They could not have it both ways. He called upon the people to decide which way it was going to be.

The people understood this too, for they responded, "We will serve the Lord our God and we will obey His voice" (Joshua 24:24).

There are three things in this incident that stand out in the context of the end-times church.

The Importance of Corporate Commitment

In many of our churches today, there is a strong emphasis on making individual commitments to Jesus. Salvation is almost exclusively seen as an individual choice, and almost all our efforts at evangelism and renewal in the church are expressed in individual terms. This is probably a reflection of the emphasis on the individual in our culture. America certainly has a tradition of individualism. We speak of people who "pull themselves up by their own bootstraps," even though this is physically impossible.

What we seldom see today is much talk of the church as being community. Yet throughout the Bible the church is not seen as a collection of individuals who come together on special days, but as people who are united in a common lifestyle.

The word that is most often used to express this in the New Testament is the Greek word *oikos*. Literally translated it means house, but carries with it the sense of a dwelling place of people. Thus, it is often translated as household, as the group of people dwelling together in the same house, that is, a family. These are people who are dependent upon one another, who look after each other and are concerned with the common well being.

So Paul wrote to Timothy, "So in case I am delayed, I write so that you will know how one ought to conduct himself in the household [*oikos*] of God, which is the church of the living God" (I Timothy 3:15). To Paul the church was not a building, or an institution, but more like a family. When we gather together, it is not for the purpose of singing a few hymns and hearing a sermon, but to encourage each other and build each other up. But being a family extends beyond the times when we are gathered together.

When I was a child my parents were insistent that we all eat dinner together. We had good times and conversations sitting around the dinner table, and sometimes we would gather afterward to play games. Most of the time, however, was spent apart from one another. Dad went to work, the kids went to school, and Mom went grocery shopping. Even when we were apart, however, we were still a family. I can remember my older brother sticking up for me when we were out playing. Family is not something you do; it is who you are.

The writer of Hebrews states,

> *Let us hold fast the confession of our hope without wavering, for He who promises is faithful; and let us consider how to stimulate one another to love and good deeds, not forsaking our own assembling together, as is the habit of some, but encouraging one another; and all the more as you see the day [of the Lord] drawing near* (Hebrews 10:23-25).

Often we speak of the times in which we meet on

Sunday morning as the time of assembling, but the meaning of that word goes beyond coming together. It means to be permanently attached. I frequently use the illustration of a bicycle, which has more meaning in places like Africa and India, where bicycles are a major source of transportation, than it does in America.

Imagine that you have just received a bicycle delivered to your door, and you are excited because now you can ride it to the church meetings. However, when you receive the bicycle, it is disassembled in a box. So you open the box and remove the handle bars, seat, wheels, frame, and all the other parts, and assemble them. It is really wonderful to have this bicycle, and so you ride it to church on Sunday morning. Later that evening you ride it to church again for the evening meeting. After you get home you will not be needing it again for several days, since the next meeting is not until Wednesday evening. So you disassemble the bike and place the parts back in the box.

Wednesday evening comes, and so you remove the parts and re-assemble them. You ride the bicycle to the meeting and come home, but since you will not need the bicycle again until Sunday, you disassemble it and place the pieces back in the box.

At this point I get some strange looks, and a few people are even laughing. When I ask why they are laughing, they respond that that is not what you do. Once you assemble the bicycle, you leave it assembled.

It is the same way with our churches. Once we are assembled, we do so in such a manner that whether it is Sunday morning or Monday afternoon, we are just as permanently attached to each other. In I Corinthians 12:12-31 Paul uses the example of a body. You never see a hand walking around by itself, but rather it is firmly attached to the wrist, the wrist to the forearm, etc.

Joshua recognized that it is important for the people to assemble and make a corporate declaration. Our confession of faith is not only personal, it is also corporate. When we stand together so that those around us hear us and we hear them, it strengthens all of us. Not only will I serve the Lord, but "we will serve the Lord." When such a confession is made publicly and corporately, we can hold one another accountable.

The writer of Hebrews goes on to point out that it is even more important as the day of the Lord approaches. In that time it is not going to be safe for the "Lone Rangers" in the church. They will not survive. Anyone who jumps from fellowship to fellowship will quickly be considered a threat by the believers.

The Importance of Obedience

It would be difficult to list all the places in the Bible where God speaks of the necessity of obeying Him. In fact, much of the Old Testament is an account of the struggle Israel had walking in obedience to God. But Israel tried to walk in obedience based upon the Law of Moses written on tablets of stone.

Obedience is a heart issue, not a legal one. God's promise through Ezekiel in the Old Testament, was that He would change our hearts of stone into hearts of flesh:

> *And I will give them one heart and put a new spirit within them. And I will take the heart of stone out of their flesh and give them a heart of flesh* (Ezekiel 11:19).

This prophecy was fulfilled in the new birth through

the death and resurrection of Jesus. When we are born again of the Holy Spirit, that spirit which God created in Adam and which died as a result of Adam's disobedience, is brought to life again in Jesus Christ. That old Adamic nature, which was sin, weakness, and death, is replaced with a new nature, which is spirit, power, and life. This is what Paul is referring to when he writes that each one of us "is a new creature; the old things [our old nature] passed away; behold, new things [our new nature] have come" (II Corinthians 5:17).

Biblically, the heart is the seat of our desires. It is what motivates us to do whatever it is that we do. With our new nature comes a new heart. We now have a new type of desire, a desire to love and serve the One who died for us.

Under the Law, obedience is primarily motivated by a reward-punishment incentive. These are laid out very clearly in Deuteronomy 28, for example. In the first 14 verses God lists all of the blessings that come from obeying Him, and in the remaining 54 verses are listed the curses of disobedience. Notice that there are nearly four times the number of verses devoted to the curses as to the blessings.

In the New Testament, the motivation for obedience is radically changed. Instead of obeying out of fear, as before, the new motivation is love. At the last supper Jesus tells His disciples that "if you love Me you will keep my commandments." (John 14:15)

It is sometimes the case that as Saturday rolls around, I would really like to go play golf, especially if the weather is nice. However, my wife has a list of jobs for me to do, and out of my love for her, I relinquish my desires to do what she wants. My motivation is that I want to please her because I love her.

This love, moreover, is not something that I have to work up. One of the outgrowths of living in the realm of the spirit, and not of the rebellious flesh, is love; not the human type of love, but agape, the God-kind of love. (See Galatians 5:16-26.) God initiates the process of loving, since He has bestowed His love on us (I John 3:1). We are merely responding to His love.

If we discover that it is difficult for us to want to obey, then we need to check our heart attitude. It is important that we spend time in fellowship with Jesus if we are to love Him. I remember that when I first recognized I loved the woman who is now my wife, I wanted to spend as much time as possible with her. I have also learned that the times I struggle the most in my attitude towards her are the times that our time of intimate communication is lacking. Like the church in Ephesus, we must return to our first love and do the things we did at the beginning.

Obedience is a choice. As Joshua called the people before him, he laid before them a clear choice. They could either choose to obey God or obey the foreign gods that were a part of the culture all around them.

Life is, in fact, a series of choices. Sometimes we wonder why "God would let this happen to me," when in fact what happens to us is the result of the choices we have made. Often, not actively making a choice to obey is actually choosing to disobey.

The word "keep" that Jesus used with His disciples in John 14:15 is a word that denotes an action on our part. It literally means to watch over. In other words, we actively seek to do His will; we ask Him what He wants us to do.

Jesus also told us that we must take up our cross

daily (Luke 9:23). When Jesus took the cross upon His torn and battered shoulders to carry it to Golgotha, He was in excruciating pain. Yet He did it willingly because it was the will of His Father.

Likewise, we sometimes do things that create discomfort in our lives, not because we want to, but because He wants us to. Perhaps this is what Paul meant when he wrote of knowing "the fellowship of His sufferings" (Philippians 3:10). These are decisions which we must consciously make.

The Importance of Hearing God

How many of us have ever made an important decision based on hearing and obeying the voice of Jesus? How many have made a decision that went against the grain of what our families and friends thought we should do?

As I was meditating on Joshua's charge to the people and his calling them to a point of decision, I was struck by their response. Not only did they promise to serve and obey God, but they pledged to "obey His voice." How can you obey His voice if you cannot or will not hear it?

I believe that hearing the voice of Jesus is one of the most difficult things with which the majority of Christians struggle. So many well meaning people go to church in order to hear from the preacher what God is saying because they have never been taught to hear from God for themselves. In fact, many Christians will deny that God speaks to them.

If you speak of the word of God in most churches, the people immediately think of the printed word in their Bibles. Yet it is clear in the Bible that the people heard God in the present tense. They did not even have a written Bible, at least not the New Testament, for it had not yet been written and compiled.

On one occasion Jesus was teaching the people and used the illustration of the shepherd.[1] Shepherding was something that was familiar to everyone in that time, but few of us today know much about it. In those days the shepherd would take his flock out into the fields to graze during the day, but it was dangerous at night. It was common for several shepherds to construct an enclosure, called a sheepfold, of thorny bushes and bring their sheep into its enclosure at night. Since there was only one sheepfold, several different flocks would mingle during the night.

When morning came and it was time to take the sheep out to pasture, the sheep needed to be separated back into the original flocks. This would be a very difficult job to do except for one thing. The sheep would learn the particular voice of their shepherd, so that all he had to do was stand outside the fold and call out to them. Those that belonged to that particular shepherd's flock would respond and leave the fold to follow him. The others would wait until they heard the voice of their shepherd.

Jesus was using this as an illustration of His relationship to those who were believers. As believers we would recognize the Shepherd's voice, so that when He called, we would know when and where to go. That is His provision for us, yet few of us have confidence that we can recognize the voice of the Great Shepherd.

If we are going to survive as a persecuted church during the tribulation, it is imperative that we learn to confidently know the voice of Jesus. It will be virtually impossible to continue the way we do things now.

I am wondering if it is not time to change how we "do church." Paul said that "when you assemble, *each one* has a psalm, has a teaching, has a revelation, has a tongue, has an interpretation" (I Corinthians 14:26, emphasis added). When you read the whole of chapter 14 you do not get the impression of one person standing up front on a raised platform expounding for 20, 30, or 60 minutes. What you see is all the people gathered, and each person participating as God gives him the revelation. One may have a prophecy, another a testimony, and another a revelation of what God is doing.

The fact is that most of us are spiritually lazy. We know that when we get to the church meeting, there is really nothing for us to do but sit there, and so we do nothing. Moreover, we know that even if we did take the time to hear from God to get a revelation or an insight into the scriptures, there would be no opportunity to share it. The one who does all the spiritual preparation is the preacher; after all, he is the one we pay to do that.

One of the things I have started to do is to read the letters of Paul, Peter, and John as they were written. That is, there was a wide-spread belief that they were living in the end-times, that the persecution they suffered at the hands of the Romans was perhaps the tribulation spoken of by Jesus. From our viewpoint they were wrong, but the result is that they wrote from an end-times perspective. So Peter writes,

> *The end of all things is at hand; therefore, be of sound judgment and sober spirit for the purpose of prayer.... As each one has received a* [spiritual] *gift, employ it in serving one another, as good stewards of the manifest grace of God. Whoever speaks, let him speak, as it were, the utterances of God; whoever*

serves, let him do so as by the strength which God supplies; so that in all things God may be glorified through Jesus Christ, to whom belongs the glory and dominion forever and ever (I Peter 4:7, 10-11).

The scriptures give testimony that each one of us in the Body of Christ has been gifted in some spiritual way. If we are going to function as an end-times church, I believe each believer needs to discover what his/her gift is and learn to function together in those giftings. Furthermore, if we seek God, He will teach us how to do this.

CHAPTER NOTES

[1] This is found in John 10:1-21.

CHAPTER 21

Gainful Pain

*Behold, I am coming quickly, and My reward
is with Me...* (Revelation 22:12).

I was speaking to a member of our fellowship recently and was trying to explain to her that it is God's plan for us to go through the tribulation. Her response was that she did not want to go through such a time. To her, as to many, the realization that there is a possibility that the church will go through persecution was bad news.

Coming to an understanding of the tribulation has been a tremendous process for me to go through as I wrote this book. The more I studied, the more I realized that what God was trying to communicate to us is good news, that there is great value and privilege of going through the great tribulation.

There is a teaching that has become popular among some churches over the last century that the rapture is going to happen prior to the commencement of the great tribulation spoken of by Jesus. In this scenario Jesus will remove the believers, leaving behind only those who have not received Jesus as Lord and Savior. The saints will not undergo any special persecution, and Israel will then be left to bear the full brunt of the fury of Satan.

That is a nice teaching, but it is one that appeals to a

church grown soft. Many people in our culture today want something for nothing. That desire is the basis for the lotteries that have become so popular and the many scams that are being perpetrated daily on thousands of people. The problem is that type of thinking in the church is of the flesh, not of the spirit.

It is like an athlete who trains hard to compete in a contest, but when the time comes for the competition, he gets cold feet. He will never know how good he is until he is tested, and neither can he receive the reward of winning unless he competes. Paul saw the analogy of the Christian persevering through tribulation to the athlete when he wrote,

> *Do you not know that those who run in a race all run, but only one receives the prize? Run in such a way that you may win. And everyone who competes in the games exercises self-control in all things. They then do it to receive a perishable wreath, but we an imperishable* (I Corinthians 9:24-25).

Athletes compete for prizes and fame that are temporary, yet they spend long hours enduring pain as they train for the contest. There is an expression that is popular among athletes: No pain, no gain. That concept carries over into the life of the saint, particularly those who are of the generation that will see these things come to pass. Look at the rewards that await those who are faithful.

We Will Have Great Joy

It is part of our lifestyle that we, as saints, have joy; it is one of the fruits of living in the spirit. However, there is a special joy available for those who are faithful in the tribulation. It is like the athlete who has been tested to the limit of his endurance and wins. Is it worth it? Just look at the athletes who compete in the Olympics and see the joy on their faces.

In the Parable of the Talents, the Master speaks to the two bond-slaves who have been faithful and says to them, "Well done, good and faithful slave. You were faithful with a few things, I will put you in charge of many things; enter into the joy of your master." In his letter, James writes, "Count it all joy, my brethren, when you encounter various trials, knowing that the testing of your faith produces endurance" (James 1:2-3).

Not only do we receive joy as we successfully walk through the trials and tribulation, but we also have a joy when those we have birthed, encouraged, and trained also are successful. Paul experienced this, as he wrote, "For who is our hope or joy or crown of exultation? Is it not even you, in the presence of our Lord Jesus at His coming? For you are our glory and joy" (I Thessalonians 2:19-20).

Joy has another important facet. The writer of Hebrews states that "for the joy set before Him [Jesus] endured the cross, despising the shame..." (Hebrews 12:2). Likewise, if we understand the joy, the immeasurable joy, that is ours, we too can endure the hardship and suffering.

Many Christians today practice a very self-centered Gospel, that God is under some obligation to give us abundant material blessings. Riches and other material blessings may produce happiness for a period of time, but it is an artificial joy. While it is true that God has promised to bless those who walk according to the principles of the Kingdom, it is also true that God expects

His people to endure and find victory and joy in everything we do.

Total Victory

One of the popular topics in many churches today is spiritual warfare. Many Christians are being taught how to do battle with spiritual principalities and powers and are seeing a measure of success. In those communities where there has been success, the leaders discovered that as long as the churches in the community remain fractured from one another, any significant victory was impossible. As they came together and put aside some of their differences, they were able to achieve some unity, and thus some success. The ultimate spiritual warfare battle, however, is yet to come.

As the Antichrist steps up the persecution of the church in his attempts to destroy it, something unexpected is going to happen. Where before Christians in different fellowships in an area were divided, they will then be forced to come together for safety and discover that the Holy Spirit will bind them into a unity. It may even happen that they forget their differences and instead concentrate on what is common. Then the emergence of the mature man that Paul writes about in Ephesians 4 will come to pass. We will see the saints being equipped for the work of service, the body coming together in a unity of faith, and believers coming into a maturity, stability, and interdependence that will result in a stronger body of Christ.

In many ways much of the book of Ephesians and particularly the section on the armor of God (Ephesians 6:10-20) is an end-times message. While many of us strive to have great victories over Satan, there is going to come a day when all we can do is what Paul says to do—

"stand firm" clothed in the full armor of God. As we stand firm in unity, we will discover three powerful weapons that allow us to overcome the enemy:

- The blood of the Lamb, which gives new life and cleanses from all sin.
- The word of our testimony, which cannot be denied.
- A love of Jesus and a hope that transcends the very love of our own lives.

Someone has said that he has read the last chapter in the Book, and we win. The enemy is caught in his own deception in thinking that he can destroy the body of Christ in the world. The amazing thing is that Jesus has given the job of overcoming Satan to us; it is our job to confront satanic forces and prevail in the name that is above all names, Jesus.

Tremendous Rewards

Look at the list of rewards as taken from the seven letters in Revelation 2 and 3 for those who overcome:

- They will be granted to eat of the tree of life which is in the Paradise of God.
- They will not be hurt by the second death.
- They will receive a new identity.
- They will walk in new found authority.
- They will be clothed in white garments and Jesus will confess their names before the Father.
- They will sit with Jesus in the seat of authority.
- They will sit with Jesus on His throne.

If those who live through the tribulation are going to be successful and faithful, they will have to be motivated. This will happen as they remember both the love of God expressed through Jesus and the rewards for faithfulness.

But there is more. As we suffer for the sake of Jesus and our testimony of His Lordship, we participate in His sufferings. As we do that we will also learn the power of His resurrection. Paul expressed it in an incomparable way in Philippians:

> *More than that, I count all things to be loss in view of the surpassing value of knowing Christ Jesus my Lord, for whom I have suffered the loss of all things, and count them but rubbish in order that I may gain Christ on the basis of faith, that I may be found in Him, not having a righteousness of my own ... that I may know Him, and the power of His resurrection and the fellowship of His sufferings, being conformed to His death* (Philippians 3:8-10).

What greater reward is there than to gain Jesus Himself!

Ruling With Jesus

Not everyone who confesses the name of Jesus is going to reign with Jesus in His millennial kingdom. At the time the tribulation begins, there will be only two groups of people—those who have already died and those who are alive. Of those who are alive and who are believers, some will become apostate and some will be faithful. Of those who are apostate, some will receive the mark and worship the image of the beast, and the others will not. Of those who are faithful, some will be martyred, and the rest will meet Jesus in the air as He comes to begin the Day of the Lord.

According to Revelation 20:5, those who have died prior to the start of the tribulation will not be resurrected until after the thousand years, and then they will face the White Throne judgment where the books are opened. (See Revelation 20:11-15.)

The apostate who worship the beast will be judged during the Day of the Lord, and those who survive that judgment will be judged when Jesus judges the nations. Either way their judgment is going to be severe.

That leaves the faithful. According to Revelation 20:4 those who were martyred because of their testimony will be brought to life to live and reign with Jesus. The other group of the faithful, those who are taken up alive to meet Jesus, will return with Him as He establishes the throne of David. So it is only the faithful who persevere through the tribulation that receive the reward of ruling with Jesus in the millennial kingdom.

Conclusion

The subject of this work has been how Jesus instructed us to be prepared for the difficult times to come. Most Christians that I have talked to about the tribulation say that they do not want to go through it. That is quite understandable, since none of us wants to suffer. However, throughout the centuries since Jesus established the Church, there have been many who considered it a privilege to suffer and die on behalf of the Savior.

We as the Church need to have a new perspective. The tribulation is not a time to be avoided or dreaded, but rather a time for which we need to be prepared. Whenever and wherever the Church is persecuted, those who decided to follow Jesus knew what the possible consequences were, and they willingly made that choice. The cost of following Jesus can be quite high, but we must be willing to pay the price. If not, we are in serious danger of falling away and of being part of the apostate church when the pressure comes.

During the last several years I have been involved with overseas short term missions, usually lasting six to eight weeks at a time. My calling is as a teacher, and my vision is to see the body of Christ built up and strengthened. Most of the work has been done in Africa, and I have faced certain dangers. Early on I came to the conclusion that in order to be a servant to the people, I must be willing to place my own personal comfort and safety aside. I do not seek out problems, but I have been in some serious situations. I have discovered that in the midst of them I am at peace.

Most believers will not face that type of discomfort, but each one needs to meditate on the possibility that they will be confronted with it. It is important for each person to make a conscious decision of the value of their life and property as compared to the value of their life with Jesus. Jesus warned us that we cannot serve both Him and wealth. The problem with the "good life" is that the love of such a life easily overshadows our love for Jesus.

Are we willing to sacrifice everything we have to maintain our testimony? Are we willing to sacrifice on behalf of others that they may live? "Greater love has no one than this, that one lay down his life for his friends" (John 15:13). Are we willing to face persecution and torture for the sake of Jesus?

These are not easy questions, but they must be answered before the time comes.

He who testifies to these things says,
"Amen. Come, Lord Jesus, quickly." Amen.
Come, Lord Jesus. The grace of the Lord Jesus
be with all. Amen.
(Revelation 22:20-21)

About the Author

Dr. Daniel Sweger has been functioning as a teacher in the Body of Christ for almost 30 years. Since 1997 he has been extensively involved in cross-cultural ministry. He has made numerous ministry trips to the nations of Africa to help equip and edify the Body of Christ there. He has also ministered in Spain, India, and Israel.

Dr. Sweger is currently teaching in the Cornerstone Bible Institute and Seminary. He and his wife Carol have been married more than 38 years and have three grown children. They are an active part of Cornerstone Church of Rockingham County, Virginia.

Over the years, Dr. Sweger has extensively studied and prepared material on many Bible subjects, including creation science and eschatology. This has resulted in two book-length manuscripts: *Created in the Image of God: Understanding What It Means to Walk According to the Spirit* and *The Coming Day of the Lord: Understanding the Prophecies About the Return of Jesus,* a detailed study of the Old and New Testament prophecies. If you have questions, are interested in any of the material, or desire to contact him to arrange a speaking engagement, please mail, phone, or e-mail:

7991 Port Republic Road
Port Republic, VA 24471
(540) 249-4833 or (540) 435-4277
or by email at: dsweger@gettingready.net
or his website: http://gettingready.net